To

thanks for encouragement

Judy Win

SandScript

A Journal of Contemporary Writing

Volume I
2003

The Board of Directors and Members of

Emerald Coast Writers

would like to thank Mrs. Sadie F. Willett

for her generous contribution to our group.

Mrs. Willett's donation is

in memory of

William P. Willett

Though we weep your death
as we harken the angels' call
that which we reaped from your life
stands above all . . .

Sadie, Gene, Dale

Sand and Sea

You wash over me
and melt away the scars
of lonely footprints,
forgotten beach blankets,
and clumsily-built castles.
Sometimes the cleansing
reveals a color-filled shell
or polished stone
that has long lain hidden,
just under the surface,
waiting for a coaxing tide.

By Evelyn J. Misok
Honorable Mention Poetry

SandScript

A Journal of Contemporary Writing

Volume 1

2003

Emerald Coast Writers

POBox 6502, Destin, Florida 32550
www.emeraldcoastwriters.org
850-654-5856

Support for *SandScript* and Emerald Coast Writers, Inc. (ECW) is provided by the generosity of our members, gifts and charitable contributions from individual readers, friends and the area businesses listed in this journal. Tax-deductible contributions are acknowledged herein.

ECW membership is open to anyone; however, membership greatly benefits writers living along or having connections to Florida's Northwest Gulf Coast. Membership information is posted online at: www.emeraldcoastwriters.org

SandScript is a yearly publication of Emerald Coast Writers, Inc., a non-profit literary organization. P.O. Box 6502, Destin, FL 32550, 850-654-5856. Order online at www.emeraldcoastwriters.org or by mail. Single copy rate: $10.00, plus $3.50 shipping and handling.

Submissions:
The literary works in *SandScript* are published as a result of Emerald Coast Writers' yearly literary contest. Contest dates, submission information and guidelines can be found online at: www.emeraldcoastwriters.org

Advertising and sponsorships:
Full page and half page ads are available in fuure editions. Exchange proposals considered. Write, call or email for rates. Advertising on our web site also available.

Permissions:
Authors in *SandScript* hold the rights to their individual works and should be contacted directly. Emerald Coast Writers, Inc. may be able to assist in locating these authors.

Distribution:
Bookstores can purchase *SandScript* through Ingram Books, 1226 Heil Quaker Blvd., LaVergne, TN 37086.

SandScript

Volume 1

A Journal of Contemporary Writing

2003

Published yearly by Emerald Coast Writers, Inc., a non-profit literary organization for writers.

P.O. Box 6502, Destin, FL 32550
www.emeraldcoastwriters.org

Publisher/Managing Editor
Julia H. Schuster

Copy Editor
Susan Farish Horn

Technical Editor
Darlene Dean

Advisors

Lynn Bowling
Diane Harris

Dawn Lyons
Ellen Martin

Readers

Carol Anderson
Lynn Bowling
Mary Brown
Mahala Church
Darlene Dean
Noel Foster
Edd Hogeboom
Joyce Holland
Susan Horn
Neil Howard
Arlene Karian

Valerie Lofton
Dawn Lyons
Janet Manchon
Ellen Martin
Katina Meacham
Delores Merrill
Joan Mucci
Pam Shirkey
Gil Stiff
Jan Whitford
Dale Willett

Judges

Dr. Vickie Hunt – *Fiction*
Vickie Hunt teaches creative writing at Okaloosa-Walton Community College and the University of West Florida. She received her Ph.D. from Florida State University. Her work has appeared in *The Chattahoochee Review, Apalachee Quarterly, Bomb Magazine,* and elsewhere, including the anthologies *Every Woman I've Ever Loved=* and *His Hands, His Tools, His Sex, His Dress.*

Amy Riddell – *Poetry*
At The University of Alabama, Ms. Riddell majored in English, creative writing and journalism. She worked as a reporter and feature writer for newspapers in three states before returning to University of Alabama for a M.F.A. degree in creative writing. Published in journals such *as College English,* the *Black Warrior Review,* and *Cen-tral Park,* among others, Ms. Riddell has taught English at The University of West Florida, Okaloosa-Walton Community College, and the OWCC Collegiate High School over the past fourteen years.

Delores Busbee Merrill – *Short Plays*
Delores Merrill is the House Manager at The Arts Center at Okaloosa-Walton Community College, Niceville, Florida. With a M. F. A. in Theater, University of Alabama and a B.A. in English from Troy State University, Delores taught Theater and Speech. She writes and directs plays: *Shoot, My Sisters This Summer, Goodbye Lenore, Vincent's Candle;* and has published numerous selections of poetry: University of Southwest Louisiana, Troy State University, Deep South Writers, New Southern Poets' Chapbook.

Judges (continued)

Randy Nash – *Non-fiction & Essay*
Having received both a B.A. and an M.F.A. in English from the University of West Florida, Randy taught English at Choctawhatchee High School for 24 years. While loving her career as a teacher, her real love is fiction writing. When in second grade, she submitted a short story to her school's writing contest and won first place. Since then, she has written sporadically and has been published in regional periodicals.

Jo Kittinger – *Children's Fiction*
Jo S. Kittinger is the author of ten books for children and numerous stories and articles, which have appeared in various books, magazines and newspapers. Her most recent books are *Going to the Beach* and *Moving Day* with Children's Press. Look for *A Lunch With Punch* and *When I Grow Up* to be released later this year. Jo currently serves as a regional advisor for the Southern Breeze region (Alabama, Mississippi, & Georgia) of the Society of Children's Book Writers and Illustrators.

SandScript

A Journal of Contemporary Writing

Acknowledgments

The Board of Directors and members of Emerald Coast Writers, Inc. would like to thank the following contributors, sponsors and friends for their support in the publication of this journal and the formation of this organization.

The Arts Council of Northwest Florida
Brooks Builders of Northwest Florida, Inc.
Carr, Riggs & Ingram, LLC
Coastal Properties of Northwest Florida, Inc.
Taco and Sandy Sanchez of Coldwell Banker Real Estate
EmeraldCoast.com
Don Gaetz
Legendary Resorts Enclave Owners' Association
Sue Lutz
Minnie Dalenburg of Pelican Real Estate
Dale Willett
Sadie F. Willett

Special thanks to Pamela A. Shirkey for the cover photograph.

A Letter from the President

It is my honor and privilege to be a part of an organization that refused to just sit around and talk about writing. The charter members of Emerald Coast Writers had a vision, and *SandScript* is the realization of their literary insight.

In less than one year, Emerald Coast Writers has traversed a vast landscape of learning — from initial formation to the publication of a journal, through research and organization to incorporation as a charitable nonprofit, from a dozen or so dedicated charter members to more than eighty members today.

I stand in awe of what we have already achieved.

With the publication of this first issue of *SandScript*, we have lived up to the precepts set forth in our mission statement, "to showcase the works of area writers" and to "assist established and aspiring writers to reach their publishing goals." In this volume, readers will discover works by some accomplished writers, as well as literary works by authors who have never before experienced the gratification of having their works published. For those authors, publication in *SandScript* is the realization of a dream.

It took talent to end up on these pages. More importantly, it took courage. The literary process of submitting your work for publication is often fraught with rejection and littered with dashed hopes, diminished self-esteem and creative slumps. These authors took on the slush pile challenge, opened their vein of creative fervor, submitted their best work and now share a plot of hallowed, literary ground, which grants their words the immortality publication affords. It is my honor to associate with writers who are willing to face the odds head-on, who give their all to their craft, who never stop learning and who, regardless of the odds, submit!

Respectfully,
Julia Horst Schuster
President, Emerald Coast Writers, Inc.

SandScript Contest Winners - 2003

First Place

Fiction:	*Homecoming*	Melita Gardner
Nonfiction:	*First Trip To A German Spa*	Ray Willcox
Essay:	*So Walt Whitman Wrote,*	
	So Wrote I	Armand Coutu
Poetry:	*Sitting With Mother*	Reg Altazan

Second Place

Fiction:	*Wedding Morning*	Judy Winn
Nonfiction:	*A River Runs Deep*	Lynn Bowling
Essay:	*Healing the Dolphins*	Pamela A. Shirkey
Poetry:	*On This December Day* Evelyn J. Misok	

Third Place

Fiction:	*Grave Water*	Reg Altazan
Nonfiction:	*Extend The Lease*	Dale Willett
Essay:	*Letting Johnny Go*	Janet Manchon
Poetry:	*Miss Hilma*	Reg Altazan

Honorable Mentions

Fiction:	*Heirloom*	Rusty Gasparian
	Sons of Cuba	Ellen Martin
	Farewell	Ray Willcox
	Seventh	Riotta Scott
	The Hand of Hattie Flowers	Armand Coutu
Nonfiction:	*Memories*	Carol Anderson
Poetry:	*Sand and Sea*	Evelyn J. Misok
	Celadon	Cynthia d'Este
	Sycamore	Reg Altazan
	Maxwell's Crossing	Don Harrison
Children's Fiction:		
	And Justice For All	Ellen Martin
	Melissa's Secret	Mahala Church
	The Orphan	M. Atwood Pusch
	Treasures	M. Atwood Pusch
Short Play:	*The Boys of Summer*	Don Goodrum

Table of Contents

Winning Entries

Table of Contents *(continued)*

Table of Contents *(continued)*

Emerald Coast Writers, Inc.
is a proud member of:

My First Trip To A German Spa

First Place: Nonfiction

When I first read the name *Baden-Baden*, I thought of a great slogan for the Chamber of Commerce. "*Baden-Baden*: So Bad We Had to Name It Twice."

Pure genius. Sometimes I amaze even myself.

Baden-Baden was the playground of the rich and famous from the 1850's up until WWI. Like most neat places in Europe, the Romans figure prominently in its history. They found the locals just using the hot springs to boil potatoes and wash socks. Clever lads that they were, they figured any place that produced wine and had the necessary ingredients for public baths could be a money maker, so they did some pretty extensive urban renewal. The locals must have loved it. They got the pleasure of becoming honorary Roman slaves, working on all the Roman projects, and not becoming dead.

Excavations revealed that the Romans heated many of the buildings by hot water from the thermal springs piped under the floors in ceramic pipes. I'll bet that made the Visigoths feel pretty stupid. They'd spent the winters being dirty and freezing there for who knows how long, and then along came the Romans and you can now be clean and warm and get a glass of wine to boot. The point of all this is that public baths were established there a long time ago and continue to this very day.

It just so happened that the oldest and most famous of the several public baths, also known as spas, was next door to our hotel. I read and shared with Paula Jane that in Europe the wearing of what we would call swimsuits is not common at the baths. The Europeans wear what we would call birthday suits. We also knew from our reading that there were hours for men only, women only, and mixed bathing and that the sessions lasted about three hours.

When PJ said, "Let's check out the baths," I assumed that she meant it like "Let's check out the town." *Nein, nein, nein,* as the Germans would say. What she meant was let's *go* to and *participate* in the baths. I did not realize this at the time.

1

We walked around the corner to the spa, through double glass doors, and found ourselves in a lobby with tables and chairs and a glass-enclosed counter like an over-sized movie ticket booth. There were brochures in various languages and all seemed to tout the wonderful benefits of a couple of hours spent at the baths. The gal in the booth must have noticed that we selected the English language brochure because she asked in English if she could help us.

Before I could say, "No, we're just looking around, so to speak," Paula Jane says, "When does the next session start, who is it for, and how much does it cost?" I was starting to feel a little nervous in the service.

She told us that the next session was for men and women, started at 1500 (3:00 PM metric time), and cost 40 DM each or 50 DM with the highly recommended soap massage. It was 1455 (2:55 PM metric) when she said those words. Taking that as a sign from God, I said, "Well, we're *way* too early for this session. Let's go check out the town."

PJ, blatantly disregarding divine guidance and my input, asked how this thing worked. "Men go up the stairs to the left, women to the right — you go separately through the first six stages then together for the next stages — just follow the instructions on the wall that are written in several languages, including English."

"There you have it," I chirped hopefully. "Let's go find some Black Forest *gateau*."

"Let's get the massage part, too," PJ replied. I could see that we were not in the same conversation.

"We don't have our swimming suits with us," I tried to hiss so that the gal behind the counter wouldn't hear. Paula gave me that look you get when you say something so stupid that even the morons notice.

And the gal behind the counter with 20/20 ears said, "You don't need bathing costumes."

If you've ever hit ice when you are driving, you know exactly how I felt at that moment. No matter how you turn the wheel, brake, or gun the engine, you are just along for a ride over which you have no control. I liberated the 100 DM from my wallet (about $60, by the way) like Lee surrendering to Grant.

"Just find a locker with a key in it, lock up your clothes, and follow the signs to station one," little Frauline Goering said cheerfully. Then she gave us a plastic chit with a number on it for the soap massage and off we went.

Paula Jane was chattering away as we walked up the stairs, but I wasn't really listening. I never intended to be here. I was thinking that even in my worst nightmares I'd never dreamed of anything like this. Who in their right mind pays thirty bucks to get naked with a bunch of strangers, German strangers at that, and prance around in various pools for a few hours?

2

So what if a massage is included? Maybe the drive up the mountain addled her mind, or the wine we sampled was drugged.

In the men's dressing room, or undressing room to be more accurate, I wondered as I *slowly* undressed, "What if this is an elaborate hoax? Maybe some sick Bavarian version of Candid Camera where innocent tourists are lured into nudity and then suddenly find themselves in front of a live television audience."

I was just about to start *rapidly* putting my clothes back on when in walked two naked German men who were chattering away as they dried off. Diabolically clever, I thought as I looked around for the hidden cameras. When they see you wavering, they send in a couple of Judas goats. A couple more German guys walked in from the entrance and started to get undressed, so I figured either they like to be naked on Candid Camera or maybe this really is a spa. I finished undressing and after giving them a decent head start, followed the signs to station one.

Station one turned out to be a shower room. The signs said to use plenty of soap and take 10 minutes. Actually, I enjoyed the shower. The soap was in liquid dispensers and smelled nice and the showers were hot and industrial strength. I may have cheated a little and stayed 12 minutes. When I left the shower for station two, I was delighted to encounter an attendant who handed me a towel and pointed the way to the next stop. I would have tipped him except for the obvious reasons why I could not. It was a big towel. I wrapped myself up like Gandhi and went into the next room.

It was the dry heat room. Patrons were to place their towels on the chairs — they were like wooden outdoor chaise lounges with no arms — and lie quietly for 15 minutes.

"Talking and loud noise are discouraged. Thank you for your cooperation," the sign read.

My initial plan was to just stay wrapped in my towel and lie down on the chair. However, that presented two problems. First, when wrapped tightly in a towel, or evening gown I'd imagine, going from the vertical to the horizontal position involves falling over and somebody yelling, "Timberrrrrr!!!" Second, those benches were <u>hot</u> and you needed your towel folded in half or you would burn your little shell pink body.

Speaking of shell pink bodies: this was the first room where I encountered other patrons. There were about 20 benches in that room and about a dozen or so guys were in there. I didn't know if these guys were "typical" Germans but they definitely did <u>not</u> fit the mold of tall, blond haired, blue eyed, muscular males. In fact, they looked much more like bears than any stereotypical image I might have had. In the main they were a barrel chested, beer bellied, dark haired, hairy, middle-aged lot. Other than the middle-aged part, I didn't exactly blend right in. Not that I was feeling self-conscious or anything.

The next stop was the "wet heat room." I never learned my Celsius to Fahrenheit conversions very well, but as I recall, the dry heat room was about 140 F and the wet heat room was about 120. I was surprised to be able to feel the difference in temperatures that warm — I'd always thought that once you got above "real hot," it pretty much felt the same from there on out. That could give those who may be hell bound a little cause for concern. It <u>was</u> humid in there. It made summers on the Gulf Coast seem arid by comparison. Ten minutes in there were followed by a five-minute (station four) shower. Sadly, I had to give up my towel after the shower.

Station five: the steam room. It was a good-sized room — maybe 30x30 feet.

The seating arrangement consisted of three tiers of ceramic blocks built up in pyramid fashion, so that the guys sitting on the top tier had their feet on the second tier. The steam was so thick that my first impression when I walked in was a scene from Dante's *Inferno*. The top two tiers were pretty full, so I just grabbed an open corner spot on lowest level. I noticed that there were showers in the corners and realized that the next station was to shower before you left the steam room.

This was a ten-minute stop and about five minutes into it, a <u>woman</u> walked over the shower in my corner! I started to cross my legs in a reflex-type reaction but even as the leg started to move, Mr. Brain pointed out that I was going to look pretty swish like that and sent a cancel message. So I sat there for a few seconds like someone doing a St. Vitus' dance. My next thought was that perhaps I should try to point out to her that this was the *men's* steam room (AKA station five) and that although it might not be readily apparent to her that some of us were men, it was readily apparent that neither was she. During this mental debate her back had been to me and I had just about decided that if I used most of the German that I did know, "two glasses of wine please...where are the rest rooms?...check please," she would get the picture.

But alas, I was too late. She turned around to face the room and I thought the poor thing was really going to be embarrassed! If anyone was embarrassed in there, it sure didn't seem to be she. I immediately began to inspect my fingernails, which had not been inspected in nearly five minutes. She said something in German, and when I looked up, she was looking at me and smiling. I smiled back and said *"einbahnstrasse"* which means 'one way street', the only other word I knew in German. She left. I was kind of stunned. Very little in my education or experience had prepared me for anything quite like this.

Nevertheless, I managed to keep at least one wit about me and observed that others who had the plastic chits were handing them to someone in the next room, then sitting down and waiting for their number to be called. Since the steam was starting to make me look like a large albino prune, I handed my chit in too.

Then I started to think and speak to the voices in my head.

I wonder who does the soap massage? A woman?

Lord, I hope not. That would be really embarrassing.

A guy?

Lord, I hope not. I don't want some guy washing me.

Have you noticed that you have used up your two most obvious choices?

Yes, I have.

But I am still thinking.

If it is a guy, I hope he's at least a straight guy.

But what kind of straight guy in his right mind would take a job like that?

Maybe they pay really big money. Right. Straight guy making good money. That must be it.

Do you really believe that?

No, but I am working on it as hard as I can.

And so it went until my number was called and I was on the verge of a nervous breakdown.

I felt *slightly* better when I went into the room and saw two massage tables. Another guy had been called at the same time and he laid down on one of the tables and rather than join him, I lay down on the other. Gunter told me (in English) to please lie down face up. That rather confirmed my suspicions that I was in no danger of being mistaken for a local boy. Step one of the process was a quick hose down of warm water.

Then Gunter grabbed a big, long-handled brush out of a bucket of hot soapy water and started brushing from my shoulders down. Had I been just slightly more relaxed than a guy sitting in the electric chair during a thunderstorm, I probably would have enjoyed it. But as the brushing got down to the bottom of the stomach area, I had pretty well decided that neither Mr. Happy nor I needed the recommended soap massage on certain regions of our anatomy. Just as I was on the verge of grabbing the brush and telling Gunter "Thanks, I'll take it from here," he shifted to the feet. Not only did I give a sigh of relief, I also giggled because the brush on the feet tickled like anything. That probably impressed Gunter, but he didn't say anything.

As the brushing moved north from the feet I was still concerned about the limits of the territorial boundaries. Needless to say, I felt much better when he put the brush back into the bucket and slapped his hands together and said, "SO!!"

I sat straight up and started to say "Thank you very much, this has been a lot of fun, if you are ever in DeFuniak Springs be sure to look me up..." but before I could get two syllables out, he pushed me back down and said, "Now for the massage." I felt like I was gaining a whole new appreciation for the expression "out of the frying pan and into the fire."

He got some kind of warm soap or lotion out of a dispenser on the wall and once again started on the shoulders and chest area. "Your muscles are tense," he said. I bit back my inclination to say I always got that way when I thought I was on the verge of being molested. "I've been under a lot of stress recently," I replied, not bothering to add that it started as recently as walking into this place. The other patron was chattering away in German to Gunter's partner. Since I did not want to encourage *any* relationship or bonding with Gunter I just stayed quiet and concentrated on wondering if the massage followed the same lines of demarcation as the brush. It did, and when he shifted to the feet I must have given a more audible sigh than I had realized.

"Good, yes?" Gunter said.

"YES," I replied with great sincerity.

The leg massage was followed by a hose down rinse off, then over onto the stomach to repeat the whole process on the back. By then I had enough confidence that the whole deal was above board and I actually enjoyed the rest of the session. After the mandatory shower it was off to the next station, station seven: mixed bathing.

Station seven was a large, brightly lit room with a pool about 20x40 feet. This is where I expected to meet Paula Jane. There were about 20 people in the pool and, since they all seemed to glance at new arrivals, I quickly got in. It didn't take long to figure out that the water was slightly less than chest deep in the whole pool, if you get my drift. But I didn't see PJ. I was fairly sure that she would be there, but since I didn't have my glasses on, I just figured that we hadn't spotted each other yet. Nonetheless, I was a little reluctant to go dog paddling from one female to the next to get within visual identification range to see if any one of them was my wife.

My solution was to just try and relax and not look like Vic the Voyeur as I tried to spot her. After about 15 minutes, the initial herd in the pool had pretty well turned over, and still no PJ. Since I had been a little slow getting started on the circuit, I concluded that she was probably ahead of me and, after the quick shower in case the spa police were watching, went to the next room.

That room had a circular pool about 20 feet across. After a quick trip around the circuit, I could see she wasn't there. So I went to the next stop, which was *another* pool, but this one was about 20x20 and only three feet deep. Still no PJ. The signs led back to the first mixed bathing pool, which was also station 12 as you made the circuit, and I knew that she wasn't there. What's a poor boy to do? I decided to just go on.

The signs said that the circular pool was cool mineral water. Patrons were supposed to walk vigorously around the circle to improve their circulation and cure all manner of ailments. If that water was cool, then the Arctic Ocean is tepid. Like an idiot, but one who will never make that particular mistake again, I jumped right on in. As the water went over my ankles, I was *almost* able to overcome the laws of gravity and fluid dynamics and jump right out again before the water got past my knees. However, my momentum was too great, and I kept right on going. Fortunately, it was just shallow enough that if one is 5'11" (1.7M) and stands on the extreme tips of one's toes, one can keep certain thermal-sensitive parts of one's anatomy from plunging into the icy depths. Despite that merciful reprieve, I could not restrain Mr. Voice from saying "Aaaaaarrrrrrrrrgggghhhhhhhh!!!!"

That drew several rather stern stares from the masochists who were vigorously walking around the circle. As I pirouetted around on my toes to get back to the edge and **out**, I smiled bravely and said, "cramp."

Even though I was only in there about 20 seconds, that water turned my legs blue and made my teeth chatter. The little shallow pool felt great because it was *warm* mineral water. Nevertheless, a knee-deep pool is really an awkward thing to deal with. If you just sit there, your out-of-the-water parts get cold. If you lay face forward, it is slightly too deep to keep your face above water while resting on your forearms. If you lie on your back with your head on the edge of the pool, your body floats and you look like you are trying to play U-boat captain. I stayed in there long enough to stop my teeth from chattering and regain the circulation in my legs, then pressed on.

There was a whole new crowd in station seven-also-known-as-12, but a slow walk around the perimeter revealed that none of them were PJ. I walked around again just to be sure. Station 13 was Dante's steam room!

Boy, was I glad that I didn't try overtly to save that lady earlier. This whole episode had been embarrassing enough as it was. This time there were a number of females in the room and they all seemed to be sitting on the lowest bench. After a trip around that circuit, I concluded that none of them were Paula Jane, although I tried to look like I wasn't looking. Since I didn't fancy climbing up the steam pyramid, I quickly cycled through the shower and out of there.

The next stop was another pool, but this one was only about 10x6 and had a banister and steps leading down into it. Something about it didn't look right. I stopped to read the sign *very* carefully. As I was reading about the importance of this last station in closing one's pores after all the previous stations had expelled the various toxins, one of the German bear-men came in and started down the steps into the pool. That first step was pretty hefty — almost to knee deep in one step. I learned a <u>great</u> new German word!

He took one more step, said that same word again, got out of there and hit the showers.

I put one toe into the water and immediately my core body temperature dropped by five degrees. Most of the ice in the world is warmer than that water. I went ahead and put one toe on the other foot in for a second, just to be symmetrical and that was enough pore closing for me — the toe pores could tell the rest of the pores later.

The last stop, after a shower of course, was really great. It was a good-sized, dimly lit room with about 40 cots arranged in a big circle. One of Gunter's buddies came in and, in exchange for the towel from the last shower, he wraps you in a warm sheet and you lie down. It was just like naptime in kindergarten! I loved it.

When I got back to the lockers, I had a fleeting thought of grabbing my clothes and taking them down to the lobby to get dressed, just to get PJ cranked up since this whole deal had been her idea. However, I could envision booth-girl calling the law and me being hauled off to the jail buck naked. I'd made it this far unmolested and I didn't want to change that statistic.

I did find Paula Jane sitting in the lobby and we had that sort of conversation that couples have when they have been running around nude with a herd of naked strangers in a foreign country. No doubt you have had that sort of conversation dozens of times, so I won't belabor it.

...And Justice for All
A Fable for the 21st Century

Honorable Mention Children's Fiction

A blaze raged through the Enchanted Forest, flames licking the treetops. Black smoke swirled and boiled high in the sky, gobbling up the usually clean, sweet air.

Wally the Weasel crouched his sleek, furry body on the ravine and gazed down at the burning forest below. He wiggled his narrow snout and smiled a sly, evil grin, exposing his long sharp teeth.

"That'll teach them for being so high and mighty," he laughed. "They deserve everything they get and more. How dare they throw me out of *MY* forest."

Reggie the Rat couldn't believe his shifty red eyes. He swished his long, skinny tail, and scurried nervously along the cliff's edge. "You've really done it this time, Wally... ruined everything. You've left the forest creatures with little hope and no security. Why did you destroy it all?"

Wally rose up on his short hind legs and puffed out his chest. "I'm king of the world... ruler of the forest." He jerked his head around and glared down at the rat. "Kings don't need a reason, and don't you forget it."

"Not much left to rule," Reggie whispered under his breath.

"What's that?"

"There's nothing left to rule," Reggie squealed in a high-pitched voice. "You've destroyed their homes, their food source, and polluted the air and water they drink. In the process you forgot one thing... it was your home... my home, too."

A chilling sneer spread across Wally's face. "We'll survive. Weasels and rats always manage to survive."

A knot twisted and rolled in Reggie's tummy; sweat poured off his brow into his beady red eyes. Wally had always been the forest bully, but this time the weasel had gone too far.

When they were kids, their pranks were mischievous and fun. But soon the fun turned mean and cruel. The gang of weasels and rats began terrorizing every corner of the Enchanted Forest, making unfair demands. "Give us money and treasures, and don't complain. Heed this warning or your children will disappear."

In the beginning, the forest creatures ignored the mean-spirited gangs, but soon children were mysteriously lost and never found. Fear spread throughout the Enchanted Forest and lasted for many years.

Wally became a very rich weasel surrounded by treasures of gold and jewels. Every day he'd dive into his riches, tossing coins and trinkets into the air.

"Power is sweet... power is mine, but I need more," he'd sing.

One spring day the families had had enough of the cruel world in which they lived. They banded together in a united front and chased the wicked weasels and rats up to the barren, rocky caves high above the Enchanted Forest.

Reggie the Rat shivered from his long hairless tail to the tip of his pointy nose, remembering Wally's evil plan. If Wally and his gang couldn't live in the Enchanted Forest, he'd destroy it so no one else could either. Yes, this time Wally had gone too far. When Eric the Eagle and his mighty force had discovered what the weasels and rats had done, their fate was doomed.

The raunchy rat scoured the smoke-filled sky, searching for any signs of the golden eagle with his proud white head and mighty wings. Reggie knew it was only a matter of time before the great warrior would hunt them down.

He wrung his hands, fearful thoughts raced through his brain. "Eric warned me not to join the weasel's gang, but I'm a spineless rat with no mind of my own. I believed everything Wally told me, took all the money and gold that came my way, with little thought of the consequences."

Reggie sighed and hung his head low. "The choices I've made will be the death of me yet. Why, oh, why have I let my fate be determined by a band of cowards?"

Tears filled his ruby-colored eyes. A deep sadness overwhelmed him for the first time in his life. Not for himself, but for all the bunnies, chipmunks, sparrows and the does raising their newborn fawns. Those innocent creatures depended on the forest to survive.

The weasels skipped about, beating drums, blowing flutes, and cheering their victory.

"Reggie," Wally yelled over his shoulder, "don't hang back. Join the celebration. This is as much your triumph as it is ours. After all, we couldn't have done it without your help."

Wally's words stabbed Reggie deep in his heart. He tucked his tail and backed slowly away from the rejoicing army of weasels and rats. He slouched low to the ground and hung his head in shame. "What have I done?" Reggie whispered to himself. "This *is* as much my fault as it is Wally's. I have to make everything right... but how?"

He lay down on the rocky mountain ledge high above the Enchanted Forest, watching the animals fleeing every which way, trying to avoid the flames and choking smoke. The blaze reached the edge of the forest and spread rapidly across the grasslands, racing toward the frightened families hovering in the fields below. Reggie's heart grew heavier and heavier.

He rolled over on his back, no longer daring to witness the horror unfolding below. He heaved another sigh. "There's got to be a way to save the animals and the forest."

He stared up into the blackening sky, praying the answer would come — but no ideas came to him. Reggie squeezed his eyes tight and wished with all his might. "Please, please someone help me save the day." But nothing or no one answered his plea — only the sound of the weasels and rats whooping, cheering, and dancing in a mad circle round and round.

High in the soot-filled sky, Reggie noticed something floating slowly down to earth. He hopped to his feet, not taking his eyes off the object gliding back and forth through the air. Is this a sign from heaven — the answer to saving the Enchanted Forest? He wondered.

Reggie scurried back and forth keeping his eyes on the small object as it danced on the air currents high above him. He couldn't, wouldn't lose it now. This was his hope, the answer to saving the Enchanted forest — it had to be. But if it is, what is it? What can it be?

Darkness clouded his vision, he blinked and the object disappeared. "No, no," he screamed, "I must have it — I must find it." Reggie frantically dashed back and forth along the mountain ledge searching, searching for the hope he needed — but found nothing.

He slumped to the ground, no longer controlling the tears and sadness filling his heart. "Please, please forgive me," he cried. "Just give me one more chance and I'll make things right... I promise."

A white feather floated down and landed on his nose. Reggie plucked the feather from its landing place, kissed it and yelled, "Hallelujah! Why didn't I think of this before? Fiona, the Dove of Peace, will help."

Reggie watched the weasels and rats hop, skip, and twirl, unaware of everything but their celebration. When he was sure they weren't looking, he tiptoed behind a rock, waiting for just the right moment to make his break and scurry into the darkness out of their view.

Free at last, Reggie scampered up the highest peak of the mountain carrying the white feather between his teeth. The climb was steep and treacherous. He slipped and slid on the loose rocks, tumbling head over heels. But he didn't care — he had to find Fiona. He picked himself up, tucked his head in determination and continued his journey in search of the Dove of Peace.

The higher he climbed, the tougher it got. Reggie gasped for air, his heart pounded in his chest, his legs ached — but he had to find Fiona. He was getting close to the top now, and nothing was going to stop him from finishing his mission.

Reggie looked up, hoping to catch a glimpse of Fiona sitting on a branch of the old gnarled oak tree on top of the mountain crest — Fiona wasn't there. His heart jumped to his throat. She must have evacuated with the others, he thought. He cupped his hands around his mouth and yelled as loud as he could.

"Fiii… ooo… na, are you home?" But no one answered. He gathered one last burst of energy and strength, and raced the final distance to the top of the mountain.

Reggie leaned against the base of the hundred-foot oak tree, trying to catch his breath. He inhaled deep and yelled her name again. "Fi… Fiii… ooo… na, are you up there? The animals in the forest need your help. Only you can save them now."

A soft whimper muttered from high above, "Go away."

"Fiona, that you?" Reggie called out. "We have to talk. I'm coming up there." His determined red eyes blazed as he climbed limb by limb up the monstrous oak tree. He slipped, almost fell, but he wouldn't stop now. It was too, too important.

Reggie finally reached the top of the tree and grabbed the edge of the stick nest. His tail and rear end swung in the breeze. He grunted and tugged, pulling himself up onto the side of the nest.

Fiona was weeping, curled up in a ball with her head tucked under her wing. Reggie stroked her velvety white feathers. "This is not the time to be sad," he said. "It's the time to act. You must find Eric the Eagle. Only he can save us now."

Fiona lifted her soft, white head from beneath her soot-covered wing, "Reggie? What are you doing here?"

"I need your help."

"This is your fault! Our friends' and family's homes are destroyed. Our life as we know it is gone." Fiona slid her head deeper under her wing. "Go away."

Reggie tucked his long, disgusting tail between his legs, and bowed his head. "I know, Fiona. But I want to make things right. It's not too late… but you've got to help! You must find Eric and his squadron of eagles. They can get rid of those scoundrels who have shaken our faith in humanity."

"It's too late," Fiona said. "Nothing will save the Enchanted Forest now."

"No, no, you're wrong," Reggie said. "Eric can summon The Great Summer Storm. With the storm, we can fight the fire that devastates our homeland. Once he brings the magical healing moisture, it will cool the dying embers. The forest will flourish once again."

Fiona lifted her wing and peered suspiciously at the rat. "How do I know this isn't one of your many tricks? You and all your wicked friends do nothing but lie, steal and cheat."

"You have every right not to trust me," he said. "But I beg you, please, listen to me now!"

Fiona wiped the soot from her beak and narrowed her eyes. "All right, Reggie, I'll trust you this ONE last time. But it better not be one of your tricks. If it is, I'll personally hunt you down and everyone in your family until you're all wiped off the face of the earth."

The weight of the world suddenly lifted from his shoulders. Reggie smiled. "Bless you, Fiona. You won't regret this. I promise."

Fiona spread her perfect white wings and lifted into the air. Reggie waved and watched her fly toward the morning sunrise searching for Eric and his squadron of eagles.

He peeked over the edge of the nest and looked down below on the mountain's ledge. Wally and his band of weasels and rats were still dancing and singing. "Victory is sweet... victory is ours," they whistled and chanted.

Suddenly, the hazy morning sky darkened in the distance. The only sound that could be heard was Whoosh... Whoosh... Whoosh.

Wally and his army of weasels stopped dancing and chanting — all eyes shot toward the sky. Their greatest fear flew high above them — humanity had been reawakened.

Wally screamed, "Run... run for your lives!" But, there was no place to hide.

A long and wide dark shadow slowly crept across the mountainside and down into the valley. Hundreds of eagles with their proud white heads and mighty wings blocked the mid-day sun. Eric and his squadron of angry birds of freedom swooped down, corralling the panicking army of weasels and rats. The frantic, squealing cowardly critters scattered here and there, but the eagles grabbed them one by one with their fierce talons, and flew high into the sky.

The birds of freedom flew over the Enchanted Forest and on the count of three, dropped the evil weasels and rats into the flames. They tumbled head over heels into the burning woodlands, putting out the blaze below.

The Great Summer Storm gathered strength, bubbled and boiled, releasing its healing shower over the blackened wasteland that was the Enchanted Forest. The moment the magical rain touched the ground, new growth sprouted, trees grew to great heights, flowers bloomed, birds sang, and a doe with her newborn fawn ventured into the fresh green field.

Eric the Eagle smiled with relief — all was well with the land. But his job wasn't finished — Wally the Weasel had escaped and still must be found.

He flew in wide circles, searching for humanity's biggest foe. He wouldn't rest until Wally was in his grasp.

Reggie saw Eric soaring above. It could only mean he was still looking for Wally. He peered down from Fiona's nest hoping to catch a glimpse of the weasel's hiding place. He stared and stared until his eyes burned and watered, but Wally was nowhere to be seen.

Something slithered under a rock, grabbing Reggie's attention. He jumped to the edge of the nest, waved his arms. "Eric... Eric, under there," he pointed and called to the eagle. "Under that rock. He's under that rock."

Eric saluted, swooped down and turned over the rock.

There was Wally coiled in a ball. His snake-like body trembled and shook, and his eyes were squeezed tight. He slowly opened them one by one, and uttered a nervous laugh. "Uh, Hi Eric," he said. "What's new?"

The great eagle grabbed Wally with his sharp, fierce talons, flapped his wings and took flight.

"Come on, Eric. Leave me alone. You know this isn't personal. Put me down!"

Eric ignored the coward's pleas.

Wally wiggled and tugged, but couldn't get loose from the eagle's mighty grip. "I've got money, lots of money. How much do you want?"

The only sound heard were Eric's massive wings cutting through the air. Whoosh... Whoosh... Whoosh.

Once again, Wally pleaded. "I'll give you your own kingdom, but you'll have to follow my rules."

Eric's steely eyes stared straight ahead, ignoring the weasel's pleas.

The twin-peaked volcano appeared on the horizon, spewing flames and molten rock. Eric flew a circle around the steaming mountain.

"You can't be serious," Wally said, his voice shaky and high. "This is your revenge? Why, you're no better than me."

Eric the Eagle finally spoke. "You're a liar and a thief and don't fight fair. You have chosen a path that's unkind to all living things. We all share this land together. Each creature that lives in this forest is different. That difference is what makes this land great. We all should respect each other's right to live the way we want. Rascals like you don't have the right to impose your beliefs on us, as we don't have the right to impose our beliefs on you. If we would join together and live in harmony, respecting each other's freedoms, we all might finally realize the true meaning of peace and love."

"But why are you taking me to the volcano? Destroying me doesn't solve your problem. Others just like me will follow."

"You're the symbol of true evil. When the volcano swallows you, the Enchanted Forest will be cleansed forever. The Great Summer Storm will renew everything that disappeared, bringing new hope and once again restoring faith in one another. You and those like you will be vanquished. No one will fear you, or the likes of you ever again.

"We will name the twin-peaked volcano Mount Humanity and with you as fuel, this burning inferno will forever belch smoke and spew flames. It will be the symbol of Justice and Freedom for all."

The Boys of Summer

(A play of one act about a life of many)

Honorable Mention Short Play

The curtain opens on a room in the Westside Hills Retirement Community in Anytown, USA. It is a minimum care facility, so there is not a great deal of medical equipment about. Furniture in the room consists of two single beds UL and UR with a two-sided chest of drawers in between. There are reading lamps either on each end of the chest of drawers or bolted to the wall over each bed. Books and personal items are also in evidence. A cedar chest is at the foot of the UL bed. The door to the hallway is DR and DL is a door leading to the bathroom. As the curtain rises, we see BUSTER DAGGET and SPENCER McLAIRY enter through the DR door from the hall. Buster is 68 years old and in reasonably good health. He is wearing a bright red warm-up suit, running shoes and a turtleneck sweater. Spencer is 70 and also reasonably healthy, though he doesn't always act it. He wears corduroy pants, a thick cardigan sweater and a plaid shirt with comfortable shoes. Of the two, Buster is the "young one" and Spencer the stodgy old man. As they enter, they continue an argument that began out in the hall.

BUSTER

(entering first and walking to cedar chest stage left)
1961!

SPENCER

(hot on his tail)
1962!

BUSTER

(turning back to face him)
1961!

SPENCER

1962!

BUSTER

Look, you senile old fool! It was *61 in '61*! Sixty-one homers in 1961! I was there, for chrissake!

SPENCER

It was *61 for '62,* you bastard! Roger Maris hit his sixty-one (bing) homers in 1962!

BUSTER

Why do you do that?

SPENCER

What?

BUSTER

That "bing" thing! We've been talking about this for an hour and every time you say "sixty-one homers", you say "sixty-one BING." What's with the bing?

SPENCER

It's for that thing they put. You know right after the sixty-one? So's you know he took more games to do it than Babe did. You know, the thing!

BUSTER

(smugly)
The asterisk.

SPENCER

Yeah, that.

BUSTER

Say it then. Say *asterisk.*

SPENCER

(with guilty defiance)
I don't want to.

BUSTER

You don't want to? You don't *want* to? You'll run around saying *bing* like

17

you was one-half of a road picture, but you don't want to say *asterisk*.
You can't, can you? You can't say *asterisk*.

SPENCER

I can so say asterkick... ah, asteritch... oh, screw you, Buster! So what if I
can't say it? You can't say onomatopoeia!

BUSTER

Look, I already told you, you Scrabble-cheating putz, that ain't a real
word! And even if it is, no one can say it except dried up old college
professors like you!

SPENCER

(blissfully)
Onomatopoeia, onomatopoeia, onomatopoeia.

BUSTER

(surprised)
How about I knock you onomato-ass? Hey, I almost said it.

SPENCER

Congratulations. I'll buy you an ice cream. Now, are you ever going to
produce this magic baseball or what?

BUSTER

Oh, right! (turns and opens cedar chest) And it is not a magic baseball, it
is a Roger Maris autographed baseball!

SPENCER

Wait a minute. You mean to tell me you have Roger Maris' number
sixty-one home run ball? Autographed?

BUSTER

(looking through chest)
'Course I don't have number sixty-one! That's in Cooperstown, surrounded by armed guards and laser beams. This is another ball.

SPENCER

(sitting on UR bed)
Another home run ball?
   (Buster says something unintelligible from within the chest.)

SPENCER

Say what?

BUSTER

I said it's not exactly a home run ball.

SPENCER

So…what is it, then? A triple? A double?

BUSTER

A foul tip, ok? My old man liked to sit behind home plate, is that all right with you? Maris popped one up over the back fence and it fell right at my feet! Man, the people in our section went nuts! I almost got my hand broke by some old broad wearing a pair of those big black grandma shoes, you remember them?

SPENCER

So you got a strike ball.

BUSTER

What?

SPENCER

A strike ball. You been making this big hairy deal about how you got a Roger Maris home run ball, but what you got is a Roger Maris strike ball.

BUSTER

It was a foul tip! And it *is* autographed and it *is* from the home run season of 1961!

SPENCER

1962!

BUSTER

It was '61!
    (sits on floor and leans against chest)
I remember it like it was yesterday…the blue sky, the green grass…

SPENCER

I prefer watching the game on television myself.

BUSTER

Television? Television is for people who aren't lucky enough to be living in New York! That's what my old man used to say. People who didn't want to sit out in the sun…

SPENCER

And that's why I like television! Too much sitting out in the sun gives you brain cancer.

BUSTER

What? Sitting in the sun does not cause brain cancer!

SPENCER

Sure it does! Look, I got two theories about life. One, is that everything causes cancer.

BUSTER

And what's the other one?

SPENCER

That everything tastes like chicken.

BUSTER

What?

SPENCER

(standing)

Sure! Didn't you ever watch the Discovery Channel or that National Pornographic?

BUSTER

National GEOgraphic.

SPENCER

Hey, every time I watch that show, they go to some island where the women walk around all day with their motherhood hanging out! To me, that's pornographic!

BUSTER

(helplessly)

What does any of this have to do with chicken?

SPENCER

Well, they go to those islands, right? And they track down the legendary Isuzu tribe of East Jesus and they eat the sacred tooki tooki bird with the traditional sauce and what do they say? They say it tastes like chicken, that's what they say!

And then, they find some guy, living for twenty years with a bunch of cannibals, eating human flesh 'cause that's all there was, you know? And what does this poor jerk say? He says it tastes like chicken!

I swear, one of these days, those E.T. aliens are gonna come flying down in their spaceships and that Dr. Spock guy with the ears is gonna take one look at us all and say, "Hmm, I'll be, they taste like chicken." Everything tastes like chicken!

BUSTER

Except the chicken in our cafeteria. That tastes like shit.

SPENCER

Yeah, but it's *chicken* shit, so there you go!
    (They laugh.)

SPENCER

Wait a minute.

BUSTER

What minute?

SPENCER

Just wait, I said. I'm doing the math.

BUSTER

Well, if you got to take your shoes off so you can count on your toes, let me know. I want to get downwind.

SPENCER

Very funny. Now, let me think. This year is 2003 and Roger Maris broke the Babe's record forty-one years ago…

BUSTER

Forty-TWO.

SPENCER

Either way, if you're sixty-eight now, then you were in your late twenties when it all happened. So if you were grown, then what's all this stuff about going to the game with your father and sitting behind the plate, huh?

BUSTER

What's the matter with you? You go to a ballgame with your old man, you gotta be a kid? Jeez… I liked the Yanks, the old man liked the Yanks, we went together, okay?

SPENCER

Alright, already. Forget I asked.

BUSTER

Well, you talk about it like there was something wrong with it Spence, that's all. Like a guy is gay or something if he spends some time with his pop…

SPENCER

Hey, watch it with the gay jokes. My Arnie is gay, y'know.

BUSTER

Yeah, yeah. Sorry.
   (a pause)
So…how's he doing with that?

SPENCER

With what?

BUSTER

Your kid. The gay thing. How's Arnie doing with that?

SPENCER

   (in a dangerous tone)
Well Buster, he's doing just fine, thank you. As a matter of fact, if this gay thing keeps doing so well, he may trade up to a transvestite thing or something. Jesus!

BUSTER

Hey, don't get all pissy. I'm just asking…

SPENCER

Yeah, well, don't. Having a kid isn't like buying a car. You can't say "Hey Lord, I want brown hair, green eyes and oh yeah, I'd just love it if he could really slam the salami."

BUSTER

Screw you, Mr. Sensitive. I got a kid too, you know. In fact Sammy called me just this morning.

SPENCER

Yeah, and how's he doing with that?

BUSTER

With what?

SPENCER

(mocking him)
Your kid. How's Sammy doing with the "being a drunk" thing?

BUSTER

(squaring off)
You sonovabitch-

SPENCER

(still mocking)
How does it feel, *Mr. Sensitive*?
(the two struggle, posture a bit, then exhausted, back off)

BUSTER

(pausing a moment before speaking, he turns away, embarrassed)
He's in a program.

SPENCER

What?

BUSTER

(turning back)
Sammy. He's in a program. You know, one of those twelve command-ment things.

SPENCER

Twelve-*step*.

BUSTER

Huh?

SPENCER

It's a twelve-*step* program. Not twelve *commandment*. It's not the Bible.

BUSTER

It is to hear him tell it. Anyway, it's hard for him, but he's kicking it. He seems happy for the first time in I don't know when, and Molly has been a rock for him.

SPENCER

Molly. That's his wife?

BUSTER

Yeah. What a good girl, that one. And pretty? She's got a smile like a spring morning. You know, in this day and age, most kids would just pack up and leave, but not Molly. She was right there through rehab, through the DT's or whatever they call 'em these days. I tell her, "Molly, you should get some rest, it does no good if you keel over yourself." And she says, "I can't, Papa B." That's what she calls me, Papa B. Anyway, she says, "This is a horse race and the prize is my Sammy's life. I can't get off of this horse 'til it crosses the finish line!" I tell you, if they ever did get divorced, I'd keep her.

SPENCER

You know who she reminds me of...

BUSTER

Yeah, I know.
   (sings)
"I want a girl just like the girl that married dear old Dad." She is the spitting image of my Emily. I met her at Yankee stadium.

SPENCER

Who? Molly?

BUSTER

No, you moron! Emily...my *wife?* I met her at Yankee Stadium.

SPENCER

I didn't know that.

BUSTER

Sure you did. It was 1958 and I'd just gotten out of the army. This was about five years before being a good American and serving your country was something to get spit on for, and my old man and I were celebrating the same way we celebrated everything, with a day at the ball park.

I tell you Spence, I don't remember what day of the week it was, I don't remember who the Yanks were playing, I don't remember who pitched or who homered or nothing like that. All I remember is going up to the concession stand for a couple of 'dogs and beers and all of a sudden, there was this vision...this angel, with blonde hair like gold and a smile like a brass band. She had on this white sundress.

You remember that? You remember how girls used to dress up when they went out of the house? Even to something as simple as a ball game? They'd wear a nice dress, maybe a hat... Emily was like that. All done up as if God had wrapped her like a present and left her for me on Christmas morning. I swear, Spencer, if I ever get so old and senile that I can't remember seeing Emily on that day... just tell them to pull the plug on my raggedy ass, cause I don't need to live any more.

SPENCER

She was a peach, your Emily.

BUSTER

A peach? She was the whole damn fruit stand and that's the truth. I still miss her.

SPENCER

I, on the other hand, was not so lucky.

BUSTER

What are you talking about? Your Abby was a lovely girl.

SPENCER

Lovely like a Doberman, maybe. When I first met Abby, I thought she was the most beautiful creature I'd ever seen. Problem was, I spent too much time thinking about the beauty and not enough time thinking about the creature.

BUSTER

So you two fought a little. Is that any reason to disrespect the dead?

SPENCER

Yeah, we fought *a little*. And Charlie Manson killed *a little*. You don't know what it was like. We were married over forty years, longer than you and Emily, and there wasn't a single day of it that she didn't pick at me and nag at me and try to make me lose my goddamn mind!

BUSTER

(shocked and concerned)
Spencer!

SPENCER

Nowadays they call it manic depression or mood swings or something. All I know is that woman had a permanent hard-on against me for over four decades and there were days I considered myself lucky to make it out of there alive.

BUSTER

Spencer, in all the years I've known you, I have never heard you talk this way. Did you take her to a specialist? A counselor, maybe?

SPENCER

What counselor? In our day, you didn't run to a shrink every time you had trouble, you didn't crawl into a pill bottle just because things were hard! You toughed it out! You picked yourself up by your boot straps and got through it! What is it my father used to say? "Hard times build character."

BUSTER

Yeah, you're a character, all right.

SPENCER

Ah, screw you again. I tell you if I'd been the owner of your precious Roger Maris baseball, I wouldn't have to look for it, Abby would've had me wearing it as a hat years ago.

BUSTER

(he'd forgotten)
The baseball!
(he goes back to the trunk and begins looking again)

SPENCER

I tell you pal, I remember the summer of sixty-two…

BUSTER

Sixty-one!

SPENCER

I remember that Abby was having one of her good spells, a good long one this time and we used to drive out to the Jersey shore and play like a couple of kids.

BUSTER

What about the brain cancer?

SPENCER

Listen, living with Abby there were worse things to be had than brain cancer. Besides, Abby in a good mood for that long was like a gambler with a run of really good luck. You don't disrespect the streak.

BUSTER

So, how was it? On the shore, I mean?

SPENCER

Oh, Buster it was wonderful. We both got brown as a couple of coconuts and I swear, it felt like we fell in love all over again. I honestly believe that our marriage lasted like it did in memory of times like that and in hopes of times like that to come. Man, we played all day and at night we'd park the kids with a sitter and go out to dinner and hold hands, and the sex! Oh my God, the sex…

BUSTER

Too much information! Too much information!

SPENCER

I was like Superman! I was like Adonis! Every night, all night long, we were like some mythological creature made up solely of arms and legs…

BUSTER

Now, there's an image I'll take to my grave.

SPENCER

Sorry. But I *will* take that to my grave. We only had maybe another two or three times like that after. It's like all of the good times that couples like you and Emily got to share every day, Abby and I had to save up and blow out like a machine gun every five or six years. And it was hard in between, walking on eggshells, trying not to set her off…

                              BUSTER
Spencer, I'm so sorry. I had no idea.

                              SPENCER
That's why I remember that year, 1962. Because it was one of the good ones.

                              BUSTER
You thinking about that year now?

                              SPENCER
   (wistfully)
Yeah.

                              BUSTER
You thinking about late at night, when you'd lie there after one of your sexual Olympic events, Abby asleep on your shoulder, the sheets all twisted up around you…

                              SPENCER
Yeah.

                              BUSTER
Your passion, as limp and shriveled as…

                              SPENCER
Hey!

                              BUSTER
Sorry. Did you ever lie there at night, Spence, and maybe turn on the radio?

                              SPENCER
Yeah.

                              BUSTER
And instead of music, did you ever tune in the game, to see how the Yanks was doing?

SPENCER

Yeah. Sure I did.

BUSTER

And did you ever hear the announcer say something like, "Wow, what a year this has been for the Yankees! All of the fame and the glory...

SPENCER

Yeah.

BUSTER

All the fuss over Maris breaking the record...

SPENCER

Yeah.

BUSTER

And then the announcer says, "Who'da' thought that the hoopla would have gone on this long since Maris broke the record *last year* in *1961?*"

SPENCER

(out of his reverie)
It was 1962!

BUSTER

1961!
            (they argue incoherently for a few more exchanges, then Buster
                                    explodes)

BUSTER

You stupid goddamned sonovabitch!
    (he backs Spencer into a corner and raises a hand to hit him)

SPENCER

BUSTER!
    (Buster pulls up short, embarrassed and ashamed of himself)
What are you doing?

BUSTER

(calmer, but still angry)
It was nineteen sixty-ONE.

SPENCER

(a little afraid, but trying not to show it)
Oh, how would you know?

BUSTER

(this is the last straw)
I *know* because my father DIED in 1961. I *know* because going to that game was the last decent thing we got to do together, that last thing we did that didn't involve *waiting for him to die.*
(he pauses, heartbroken while Spencer looks on in helpless silence)
My old man loved the Yanks, 'you understand what I'm saying, Spence? My mom used to say that if my old man had to choose between her and his team, she wasn't sure she'd like his choice! It was almost as if he was waiting for the record to be broken so he could die *knowing*, do you know what I mean? Like whether or not the Babe's record could be broken and who broke it was something worth taking to the grave. And he loved Maris, absolutely *loved* him! Everybody else was "Mantle this, and Mantle that," but my old man loved Roger Maris. Thought he had class, y'know?

SPENCER

(he can't help getting his two cents in)
I was always a Mickey Mantle fan myself.

BUSTER

Mantle? Are you kidding? Mantle was a *showboat*, a big party-boy who let his *little bat* do all the thinking for his *big bat,* you know what I'm saying? I mean, Mantle could play... nobody's ever gonna say Mantle couldn't play, but God reached down at birth and gave that boy an arm full of lightning and he didn't *respect* it, didn't take care of it. That's why God took him out of the race for the record, why he messed up Mantle's hip, so that the record would be held by a guy who had respect for what God had given him.

SPENCER

Yeah, but didn't all of Maris' hair fall out?

BUSTER

Sure, from the *stress!* Maris wasn't built for the spotlight, all the photographs and the looky-loos and the parasites that can chew up a good man right in front of your eyes! The way he can just waste away in front of your eyes 'til he's nothing but a dried up old leaf on the sidewalk!

SPENCER

Are we still talking about Maris?

BUSTER

My old man was getting the chemo, you know? And back then that shit really tore you up. He used to joke that him and Maris were in a race to see whose hair fell out first. He used to save all the bits he found on the pillow or in his hairbrush and put them in this little plastic bag. I asked him once if he was saving up to make Maris a wig and he just looked at me with his red eyes and that 'grin and bear it' smile he used to wear, and said to me, "Buster, when you don't have much of yourself left, you have the hardest time even letting the smallest pieces go." He died about a week later. So fast... Maris hit number sixty-one in September and my old man was dead and buried by Christmas.

SPENCER
(putting a hand on his friend's shoulder)
Buster, I'm so sorry.

BUSTER
(collecting himself)
Anyway, that's how I know that Maris broke the record in sixty-one, 'cause my dad reminds me every time I go visit him.

SPENCER

Ok, Buster. You win. It's sixty-one. I must be mistaken.
(pause)
But look, are you ever going to show me this ball? What'd you do, wrap it up in the Shroud of Turin and hide it in the Lost Ark or something?

BUSTER

Right, right, the ball. Hang on a sec...
(rummages furiously through trunk)
Aha, here it is!
(produces worn old baseball)
See the autograph? "Roger Maris."

SPENCER

Let me see that.
    (takes ball and inspects it closely)
"Rodney Murray."

BUSTER

What?

SPENCER

The autograph. It doesn't say "Roger Maris," it says "Rodney Murray."
You got gypped.

BUSTER

Give me that!

SPENCER

    (handing over ball and laughing)
I'm just kidding. It says "Roger Maris," all right. That's pretty sharp,
Buster. It must be a nice keepsake.

BUSTER

    (looking at ball and thinking)
Oh hell man, it's just a baseball. The stuff worth keeping, I put in here.
    (taps his chest)
    (the two sit for a moment, lost in their private thoughts
and recollections)

SPENCER

So...maybe we should talk about something else.

BUSTER

Sure, what would you like to be wrong about now?

SPENCER

I know! You can't argue with me about this! The greatest comeback of
all time...Muhammad Ali!

BUSTER

Cassius Clay.

SPENCER

I know he was born Cassius Clay! But he changed it Muhammad Ali.

BUSTER

Yeah, Harold Jenkins changed his name to Conway Twitty too, but his driver's license still said "Harold Jenkins."

SPENCER

What are you saying, that "Muhammad Ali" was a stage name? He changed it when he became a muslim! It's a religious thing.

BUSTER

Did his momma name him Muhammad Ali?
    (a beat)
Then it ain't his name. I wonder if they're serving dinner yet?
    (gets up and moves to exit DR)

SPENCER

The man was the heavyweight champion of the world almost longer than you've been alive, I guess he can call himself whatever he wants! Muhammad Ali!

BUSTER

Cassius Clay!

SPENCER

Muhammad Ali!

BUSTER

Cassius Clay!
    (their argument fades out as)

CURTAIN.

Heirloom

Honorable Mention Fiction

He buried her in the backyard under the sheltering arms of the Live Oak tree. He wrapped her frozen body in the well-worn patchwork quilt. He sat on his haunches rocking back and forth like a mother with babe in arms. Fourteen hundred different pieces of fabric, a Charm Quilt or Beggar's Quilt they called it. No two pieces of fabric were the same. A single template repeated over and over again. This was the inheritance. Joshua, Kim's son, would lie in bed and search the quilt, hunting for a repeated fabric. It was the blanket he had been wrapped in the day he came home from the hospital. Tradition, they told him. His mother, his grandmother, his great grand-mother and so on. "I know she'll be pissed but I don't care. This is her fault — all her fault," he screamed into the darkness of the storm.

We admitted we were powerless — that our lives had become unmanageable.

When Kim walked into her apartment from work, the light on the answering machine was blinking. She heard her son's voice, "Mom, Mom, I need you," and then he hung up. He never called. Usually he tried to avoid her. Something's wrong, I just know it, she thought. Why doesn't someone answer the phone? Where are they? I can't stand this much longer. Damn it! Do I go over there or not? No one answers the phone at the house and I can't get his father at his office either. That sick feeling that had begun in her stomach when she first heard her son's voice on the answering machine now spread through every pore of her being like a deadly virus and an all too familiar friend.

Finally her husband answered the phone. "I found him out back crying and rocking Patches' body in his arms. He had her wrapped in his baby blanket, and then I helped him bury her," Larry said to his wife as she gripped the phone a little tighter. She could imagine father and son standing together, looking down at the grave, with arms around each other's shoulder.

"How could you let him do that? That's a handmade quilt. You have to go dig the cat up and get the quilt back. It's supposed to be passed down from generation to generation. You know how old and delicate that quilt is. What in the world were you thinking?" Kim asked her husband in that tone of voice — the one that he hated so much, the one he said sounded like she was talking to a child. Another one of those damn habits and patterns she was trying so hard to break, like chewing the inside of her mouth when she was upset.

"I wasn't thinking," Larry answered. "You come over and tell him he has to dig her up because the blanket is an heirloom. Besides, he asked to see you. He wants you to come over; after all, you're still his mother, aren't you?"

"That isn't fair, and you know we both made this decision to separate for the good of us all." She stopped herself from slamming down the phone. "I'll come over to the house as soon as I can." Patterns were like looking for that one last illusive piece to the jigsaw puzzle. Would it ever be finished? Would it ever be dead and buried? This insidious, cunning, baffling sickness?

Came to believe that a power greater than ourselves could restore us to sanity.

He had come home from work as soon as his youngest son had called him — a first, she thought. Recently she had learned to think before letting her tongue get away from her, but didn't always succeed. They had been out back burying the cat when she called. Patches was dead, ripped to shreds by a pack of marauding dogs, a pit bull and his companions. Destroyed like their lives from this generational disease.

Father and son had been looking for the cat for two days. Somehow she had managed to get out into the storm. The neighbors asked Joshua if he had an orange and black colored calico cat with a white chest and white front paws. He did have a cat. He was six when his older brother brought her home for him. The cat was a wild stray orphan in need of rescue and looking for a mother. Now, eleven years later, the Humane Society brought her body to him.

Made a decision to turn our will and our lives over to the care of God as we understood Him.

They had tried to beat the weather and get home before the hurricane hit. Twenty-eight days, exactly, he had been gone, in treatment, working *The Program*. They rode in that brutal silence that seemed to swallow them whole for twelve hours straight. They stopped only when necessary for potty breaks and hot coffee, or a stale snack from the vending machines at the roadside rest areas. Even these short breaks became cause for dissension. She was sick of all kinds of counseling and therapy — marriage, group, family and individual. Confront denial head on, they said. Rip them open, take out their insides, and send them home but like Humpty Dumpty: no one could put their family back together again. Ah, the things that are handed down from generation to generation.

Made a searching and fearless moral inventory of ourselves.

Patches was an inside cat with no claws, no way to defend herself. "I suppose this too is my fault for not being there, for being the one who left. Joshua knows she will only come if I call her," whispered Kim to herself in that faraway tone.

"No one is talking about blame here. I simply found him out back crying and rocking her in his arms. He already had her wrapped in his baby blanket when I got there, and then I just helped him bury her," Larry said. Kim pictured her husband on the other end of the phone with his brow furrowed, face dark and bedroom blue eyes angry at being challenged.

"Couldn't you put her in something else? That's a handmade quilt. You could have suggested something like a cardboard box. You need to go dig her up and get the quilt back. That is one of the few things I have left of my mother's. "

"You come over and tell him he has to dig her up because the blanket is an heirloom," Larry said, as he sucked on his pipe and blew smoke into the receiver. "Don't you think that maybe it's time to give up a little control? Live in the present? One step at a time, they say — one day at a time. Give it a try, why don't you?"

Admitted to God, to ourselves and to another human being the exact nature of our wrongs.

Why now, when things were beginning to improve, and why the cat, she wondered? The one thing he could love, trust, talk to, and the one thing it seemed that was safe for them to talk to him about. Patches was the one who guarded her son's domain, protected his interests. The once passive cat, who later attacked anyone who crossed the threshold of Joshua's bedroom while he was away, was dead. At the start, Patches had been Kim's pet but even the cat had come to treat her like the enemy.

I'm his mother. I want to be the one who comforts him and holds him. But I don't live there anymore. I'm the outsider — I'm the bad guy, the one who sent him away to treatment. She could still hear his voice the day they took him away, and remember the look of hatred in his eyes. "I will never forgive you for this. I trusted you and you betrayed me," he said. And he had kept his word. He wouldn't let her touch him, hug him and certainly he never called her at her apartment or office, not for any reason. Not even when they let him make his weekly phone call.

The disease that consumed them all — hungry, devouring — like a rip tide pulling them down and under and still would not let them out of its grip.

Were entirely ready to have God remove these defects of character.

Then, finally, when silence and locked doors and brick walls became the norm, she knew it was time to go – that, and the burned pieces of her favorite blouse she found in a hole in the back yard under the old oak tree. They had discussed who should stay, who should go, but they agreed that together no one would survive living in the same household. Divided, maybe the disease would not conquer.

Humbly asked Him to remove our shortcomings.

"He needs you," her husband had said, in that little boy voice. Not anymore, she thought. He is supposed to go to college next year. Kim knocked on the door of what used to be her home too. She was concerned about what might occur and braced her body for the onslaught. Scenes of other times flashed through her mind. Fist-sized holes in his bedroom wall from the day he left. She remembered his belongings, broken and destroyed, on the bedroom floor. And there was Patches standing behind him, hissing at her right along with her son. But this quilt is an heirloom, she thought to be handed down someday her grandchild, his child, would inherit this worn patchwork quilt, this Charm Quilt.

Made a list of all persons we had harmed, and became willing to make amends to them all.

She knocked again and Joshua opened the front door. "Mom, Mom," was all he could say. It was then that the image flashed through her mind of the little boy in his first homemade Halloween costume, a bright orange pumpkin outfit. He was supposed to be born on Veteran's Day, but it was a high-risk pregnancy and he was born early, sunny side up, with umbilical cord wrapped around his neck.

His older brother and sister thought it would be cool if the new baby were born on Halloween. "We could call the baby Batsy if it's a girl and Frank N. Stein if it's a boy," they said. Their grandmother took them out for Trick or Treat, and Kim went to the hospital.

Made direct amends to such people wherever possible, except when to do so would injure them or others.

At the meetings, they talked of sponsors, the disease, detachment, denial and the elephant in the room that everyone ignored. "Hell, we have a whole circus in the house," she would say to them. And if someone brought up the river called Denial, one more time, she knew she would scream. The nights were the worst, waiting, listening for him and then pretending to be asleep when he finally arrived home. Confronting him in the light of day when he was sober, making sure she was standing across the room from him, close to an exit when she spoke to the boy who now towered over her.

Continued to take personal inventory and when we were wrong promptly admitted it.

When he was little, he thought it was the neatest thing in the world to have a special holiday birthday, until fifth grade when Shelley Ryan told him he was the devil's child. That happened right after they moved south to the Bible Belt. He kept the blanket on the foot of his bed even then, and that's where the cat slept, curled up on the foot of the bed on top of the patchwork quilt.

Sought through prayer and meditation to improve our conscious contact with God as we understood Him, praying only for knowledge of His will and the power to carry it out.

She remembered one of their first group sessions at the treatment center. They sat in the middle of the room in chairs facing each other, with the other families seated around them. When it was her turn, she sat in a chair across from her son. He wouldn't make eye contact with her, and she felt only the cold seeping into her bones. "This helps break through the denial," the therapist said. Sure, she thought, drag out all the family secrets and skeletons in front of strangers. It's the parent's fault, that's what this is about, never mind that her son had lost 40 pounds and saw and heard things that weren't there, and that they slept with their bedroom door locked. Only it was the therapist who did the confronting. He challenged Kim on her anger and codependency issues. Joshua, her son, had defended her then, protected her as if he were the mother bear and she the cub.

Once he had loved planning his birthday parties with her. They would choose a different theme every year in keeping with his costume. Some people, when they discovered that his birthday was on Halloween, found it amusing to ask her if he were a Trick or a Treat. Usually she responded by nodding her head, smiling with that knowing look, and simply said, "Yes."

Having had a spiritual awakening as a result of these steps, we tried to carry this message to others and to practice these principles in all our affairs.

She thought of the last night before he left for the treatment center. He had wanted to talk to her. They had sat on the floor outside the entrance to his room, side by side, shoulders touching, backs against the wall, the quilt wrapped around them. He spoke of his friends and Dylan who was in the hospital because of stomach problems and seizures. They had skipped school together, and she could sense the fear laced around his words. She heard the vulnerability in his voice. He needed her then, wanted a mother. Patches lay in Joshua's lap and he stroked her gently as he spoke. She promised him he could stay home from school the next morning, and she thought of the Steps and the Slogans and knew what she would do. She tucked him in bed that night and folded the quilt neatly on the foot of the bed for the cat, turned out his light, closed the door, walked to the phone and made the call to the treatment center. This, too, shall pass, she said to herself as she hung up the phone and waited for morning.

On This December Day

Second Place Poetry

I'd love to talk to you today,
On the back porch, our sweaters on,
And feed on toast and orange juice
And the day's first smiles,
Our breath puffing clouds
Into the morning air.

I'd love to talk to you today,
Sunglasses perched on our noses,
And munch on grilled cheese sandwiches
And stories from yesterday,
Our laughter startling the sparrows
Into the bright noon sun.

I'd love to talk to you today,
Comparing socks and favorite robes,
And feast on wine and good bread
And plans for tomorrow,
Our whispers drifting low and sweet
Into the starry night.

I'd love to talk to you today
To slip into your silken gaze,
And sample the salt of skin and tears
And dreams too soon abandoned,
Longing with each word left unspoken
For just one more day.

Homecoming

First Place Fiction

I closed my eyes and rocked to the train's rhythm. It had been six years since I traveled these curves toward Zagreb, my hometown, for the first time after I had left home in 1970 following my mother's death. Yet the rhythm stayed etched in my mind like my mother's lullaby. I was coming home, now a new country, Croatia, independent for the first time in a thousand years.

"Mind you, Veronica, there will be war," my oldest friend Mira, her usually deep voice a pitch higher, had warned me when I was last here, in 1989. "Croats are tired of Serbian exploitation."

She was right. The war broke out two years later. Serbian bombs fell even on Zagreb and almost destroyed Karlovats, a city just an hour away by bus. I lost touch with Mira. For two years she hadn't answered messages I had left at the hospital where she worked. When she finally called, she suggested I come to Zagreb and write a piece for my magazine about the war and the Bosnian refugees. All Europe was dealing with them.

Mira had been my home, the only friend I had kept, my friend since fifth grade. After school, we had roamed the city together, laughing and pulling pranks, her long black braids bouncing, brown eyes sparkling. We would ring door bells and hide when heads appeared in windows and on balconies, scolding and even cursing. If I hadn't stopped her, she would have thrown a dead rat into somebody's doorway or tossed water on passers-by from her third-story balcony. But she stopped to comfort a lost seven-year-old boy and helped him find his mother.

When we turned 18, we both dated Vlado, the budding rebel and politician. He chose Mira instead of me, so I hurled insults at Mira that still echoed in my ears thirty years later. But after Vlado dropped her, we became even closer, as his actions convinced both of us men were weak and unreliable. Those were the sixties and we were feminists. Mira never married and became a doctor, while I stuck to scribbling and foreign languages. Now she would be my guide, my *cicerone*, in the born-again Croatia.

I relished the train's quiet sway through open spaces, the smell of autumn hay unalloyed by the smoke of coal-powered trains, now retired. I was brought out of the reverie by prolonged squeals and a magnified echo that announced changing of tracks and a big station. Even through closed eyes, I sensed the shift in the quality of the night, the lightening of the darkness, and soon recognized Zagreb by the number of twists; I knew the streets we passed by the tattoo of the wheels; I smiled.

As soon as the train slowed, I reminded myself I was not here to day-dream but to do a job. I stuffed copies of *Ms.* magazine in my pocket and sat up straight. As the train rounded the familiar long curve, the big green sign came into view, its white letters announcing Zagreb, Croatia. The year was 1995, and the Croats had won the war of separation from Yugoslavia. Nothing would ever be the same.

When the train slowed, I was ready at the door, suitcase in one hand, my overnight bag in the other, the passport, the wallet and the press card in my pocket. Just in case, even though I knew the Croatian authorities would not stop me or search me. I pushed the door open but was repelled by the stench on the platform: stale food, sweat and urine. Travelers hurried toward the exits, avoiding crowds of Bosnian refugees, mostly women and children. The pale, emaciated figures sat and lay on benches, shuffled around or leaned against the walls covered in soot and grime. I put down my bags, extracted my Nikon and pointed it at them, deliberately and slowly recording everything. The women paid no attention to me, while their children clung to them whining. Their lifeless hair hung in clumps, and their soiled clothes seemed inadequate against the autumn winds. A woman approached me with her hand out, and I gave her a fifty-kuna bill, less than ten dollars. Children turned and stared, fingers in mouths, and in the corner of a bench, a black-haired woman regarded me with huge burning eyes.

Suddenly a stout man appeared next to me, tipped his porter's cap, grabbed my suitcase and hurried off toward the exit.

"*Kurva Americka*," he mumbled. American bitch.

The sound of my mother tongue splashed me like cold water. I was home.

"Hey, *prijatelju*," I called after him in Croatian, "wait a minute."

Startled, he stopped, then slowly turned around, saying, "Why do you photograph them, let everybody see our shame?"

"*Svijet mora...* " I tried to explain to the porter that the world ought to know, but stopped mid-sentence. His flashing eyes spoke of hurt pride, offended dignity. He threw down the suitcase and spat, cursing the American Croats who failed to understand those left behind.

"*Da ti se jezik osusi*," may your tongue dry out, he added and walked away. Immediately, next to me materialized a young boy wearing a cap advertising Hotel Esplanade, his sharp elbows protruding from a striped sweater.

"You going to Esplanade?" he asked in English.

"Why are all these refugees here?" I asked him, handing him my suit-case.

"No room in camps," he shrugged and hurried through the building. Outside, the noise assaulted me. Even at nine in the evening, crowded trolleys clanged, cars honked, people shouted, diesel fumes permeated the air. The boy elbowed his way through a group of loud, gesturing people. They stopped, glared at him and swore. Somebody shook a fist in his face, so I tried to skirt the groups. At the curb across the street from the hotel, I had to wait a good ten minutes before the traffic let me cross. Six years earlier, Zagreb had been a quiet provincial city.

The Hotel Esplanade hadn't changed much, however: no ill-smelling Bosnians here, no vacant-eyed crowds. I was relieved when I finally reached my room and tipped the elevator boy. More luxurious than accommodations in the Hilton or even the Marriott hotels back in the U.S.A., my room featured a feather bed, a baroque chandelier and prints of Croatian primitives on walls. I opened the window to air the room. Under the window, on the terrace, a local band rocked. Tall poplars and maple trees, ablaze with fall colors, surrounded the terrace and muffled the sounds of trolleys and trains. Judging by the crowds gathered under my window, young people from Zagreb and elsewhere still flocked here to dance. Too tired to join in, I was in bed by ten-thirty.

***

I woke at dawn to unfamiliar sounds of trolleys and car horns. No pedestrians as in the old days. From a distance, I heard trolley wheels whining on turns, brakes squealing, people shouting and cursing. Stretching on the soft bed, too soft for my American taste, I thought of the important role the crowded streetcars, their open red and blue cars, had played in my youth. I could smell the heat of summer days and long trolley rides to the beaches of the Sava River where I had discovered muscled young men in tight, bulging swimming trunks.

But that was a long time ago. Now I was here to report on Bosnian refuges, the Yugoslav fratricidal war, and the Serbian bombs, which had almost hit President Tudjman's palace. I made a face at myself in the mirror across from the bed, sighed and got up. Since it was too early to call anyone, I decided to start the day with a walk. I showered and pulled on my jeans.

Across from the hotel, I saw a few scrawny women in baggy harem pants called *dimlije,* or in dirty dresses that hung loose from bony shoulders, scrounging among plastic garbage bags left on the curb. Back in America, women power-walked; these women shrank from glances and scurried sideways. Even bag women on Seattle streets walked erect.

The streets in Zagreb depressed me the most. The city used to keep them clean and swept every morning, while now, paper and tin cans blew around wheels of cars parked on sidewalks. I stepped on a waxed carton and thick juice leaked out, probably apricot, my favorite. Black dust lay next to basement windows, smelling of cat urine, and all buildings were black with pollution.

Very soon, streets came to life. School children, satchels on backs, hurried by in groups. Women headed toward Jelachich Square, probably to the market. They carried reticules or pulled the netted bags on wheels to help in the daily ritual of buying supplies. I reminded myself to stop at the market, take some pictures of the big red umbrellas over displays of everything, from fish and cheese to exquisitely crafted leather goods. The picture would serve as a contrast. I was surprised to see so many well-dressed women, many of them in dark slacks or narrow skirts and stacked shoes, attempting to imitate the latest Italian fashions. I looked at my comfortable old sneakers and faded jeans and decided to go back to the hotel. In order to avoid stares, I should dress according to the local standards. Dressed in trendy clothes, Zagrebars thought they were cosmopolitan. Gone were the days when my friends and their children had wanted to buy my worn American jeans.

At the hotel, I called Mira.

"Finally, *srce moje*," she exclaimed.

She always called me "dear heart," a term of endearment that brought back the deepest and oldest feelings, the time when I still sucked my thumb and hung on to my mother's skirt. My mother, long dead...

"Veronica?" Mira broke the silence.

"Finally here," I managed to say after clearing my throat.

"Are you okay? *Milo moje*, it is hard to come back to the old city so ravaged and so dirty! Ah, well, our cross. At least you're here to witness history in the making."

Then she added in a matter of fact voice, "Meet me on Jelachich Square, under the horse's tail. The old rendez-vous place, the statue, remember? But don't hurry, eat breakfast. See you at ten."

She was always considerate, even in a rush. I collapsed on my bed and burst into tears, something I hadn't done since my divorce. All because of those old endearments I hadn't heard since... well, since my last visit.

After a quick breakfast, a hard roll, raspberry jam and café au lait, I changed into a skirt and sweater and hurried along Zrinjevac, teeming with passers-by and clanging street cars so crowded people hung out on steps.

A rickety red car almost tipped on a sharp turn. Cafés were full, people waiting by the doors to take the places of those who were leaving. Strong smells of coffee and cigarettes wafted out when the doors opened, and I caught glimpses of glass counters full of pastry, everything from éclairs to fruit tarts. Always money for *kafich* and the sweets, Mira had written, even when Zagrebars diet consisted of potato soup and tripe. No money for leaky roofs, either, I thought, looking up at patchwork shingles.

The traffic and noise increased as I approached Jelachich square, the trolley intersection. Groups, mostly women, stood on the sidewalk talking and gesturing. Eyes downcast, I fought my way through, trying not to notice the beggars as they went by, empty hands outstretched, until banging on my left attracted my attention. A little girl, one leg a stump, sat on the ground, her right hand frozen in front of her, and banged her head against a loose aluminum drainpipe. The pipe tattoo was louder than all the streetcars and vendors. I put a bill into the small hand, but the hand didn't close and the drumming didn't stop.

Suddenly I found myself pulled away and Mira's voice whispered in my ear, "Don't give them anything. They just get used to begging. We have jobs for them."

"Mira," I grinned and gave her a big hug, then realized what she was saying. I stepped back.

"What do you mean? Why not give them something?"

"Trust me. It is a bad habit." She was a new, matter-of-fact Mira.

My joy at finally seeing her won out. I took her by both arms and exclaimed, "Oh, Mira, let me take a good look at you."

She tried to smile, but the twist of her mouth only distorted the thin face; permanent worry lines deepened. Her big brown eyes flashed with a kind of force I had not seen before, erasing their former twinkle and readiness to laugh. Even her black curly hair, cropped short, no longer bounced. Her nails were chewed to the quick. She wore a pale yellow uniform, which made her face sallow.

"Well?" she asked.

I shook my head. "I think you should come home with me to America for a while. Put some flesh on you and a smile on your face."

She shook her head. "Wrong time. Too much work to do. Let's take the funicular uptown."

She took my arm and pulled me toward Ilitsa, and the old creaking lift pulled by a cable on steep tracks. It started slowly, then shot up. Red house tops tilted toward us, then the fields beyond and finally the silver streak of the river Sava, dividing the old stately houses from a forest of high rises in New Zagreb, softened by trees in colors from yellow to bronze red. My camera finger went wild, from left to right, until Mira reminded me we had an appointment. At that moment, tall smokestacks belched thick smoke, which curled and hid the river and most of the New Zagreb.

"Hurry," Mira said, pulling me by the arm, so I missed my shot.

"Where are we going?" I asked

"To the Lyceum, our old school, remember?"

We said nothing more until we reached the St. Catherine Square. The pock-marked gray building of the Lyceum loomed on the right, covered with lichen and grime. The quaint Renaissance style church of St. Catherine in front of us shone in the sun.

"Tudjman is trying to renovate the Old Zagreb," said Mira pointing to the newly scrubbed church. She sounded dismissive, but a bit of the old spark shone in her eyes.

Mira entered the arched entrance of the school and pressed the bell, which rang deep inside the building. The entrance smelled of must and rotten vegetables. Leaning against the meter-thick wall, I asked, "Do teenagers still kiss here?"

Mira nodded.

Closing my eyes, I could feel the cold wall pressing against my back and Danko's kisses on my lips. I shivered and thought how lucky were American teenagers who did their groping in back seats of cars. Abruptly, a nun opened the door, nodded to Mira and me and led the way. She wore a short black dress and a gray apron, which emphasized her scrawny figure. Her hair was tucked under a black cap. I did not see her face.

She led us into the first classroom. Here, young women, most of them pregnant, sat on the floor under tall windows; some sat on school benches and munched coarse bread and cheese. Across the hall in the bathroom, four of them washed clothes at stained, old sinks with barely trickling water. Startled by gaunt, staring faces, I wanted to ask questions, take photographs, but Mira shook her head and led me to the basement, to a makeshift kitchen where two young women washed tin pots and plates in a rusty tub.

Then one of them looked up; a pair of blue ferocious eyes slapped me. Even her thin brown hair seemed electrified, as if it were standing on end. Under a shabby tee-shirt, a small, round belly pooched out, incongruous above long, skinny legs. She couldn't have been more than fourteen or fifteen. But something else in her face struck me, something familiar that went back to our school days. When I touched the girl's arm to make her look up again, suddenly I saw Emina, the only Moslem girl in our class, the girl we all had envied for her good looks and nice clothes. She had uncles in America.

Tallest in class, Emina had glided on long legs, her honey-blond hair flowing down her sloping shoulders. The exquisite head rested serenely on the neck as long as Queen Nephertiti's. The oval of her face was more perfect for high cheekbones and slightly slanted eyes. She fell in love with the poet Marko Radich, who attended seminars at our school when the University of Zagreb ran out of space in its buildings. Tall and hunched over, Marko dreamily followed Emina with his eyes, then began courting her. When he finally asked her out, we all covered for her. Moslem girls were forbidden to date, and if her parents had found out... Well, we weren't sure what would have happened, because Emina took fright and stopped going out. Later, we heard one of her cousins from overseas wanted to marry her.

Stepping back, I pointed the camera at the girl, but Mira stopped me. "The nuns would object," she whispered.

"Whatever happened to Emina?" I asked, lowering the Nikon.

Mira looked straight at me in that disconcerting way she had acquired. "She has Emina's eyes, doesn't she? Emina married a merchant from Tuzla and had a miserable life. But I don't know if she had any children."

"Our Moslems here were so secretive. And how old is this girl? Just a child."

"A child of fifteen," sighed Mira. "Her name's Suleima."

"Can we take her out for coffee or something?"

"I'll ask the nuns."

***

Mira and I took Suleima, scarf wrapped around her head and neck, to the City Café, bathed in blue cigarette haze. The low buzz of conversations stopped and I felt more than saw the scrutinizing glances that followed us. The burgers there weren't used to seeing little Moslem girls in cafes. The only table we could find was on the second floor. Thoroughly unnerved, I ordered a cheese sandwich for Suleima, then resorted to my usual defensive behavior, chattering, while Mira studied reports spread out in front of her and Suleima devoured her sandwich. All of us drank strong espresso. Finally I stopped talking and looked around me, remembering all the evenings we had spent there as students deciding the fate of the world. Oh, we were brave then, throwing out phrases like "We have the choice," or "We will boycott Tito's decisions," through blue haze while we drank thick, sweet Turkish coffee, poured from a brass ibex.

A change in Suleima jolted me out of reverie. Her cheeks flushed pink and her eyes even more ferocious, she sat up straight, like a schoolgirl, and stared at me. Suddenly, she stuck her tongue out, licked her lips and spat.

"Iblis' child, this," she broke the silence, patting her belly.

A devil's child.

"You're pregnant, aren't you?" I asked, startled.

"The devil came to me, to Mother and to Naida. Only twelve Naida

47

was, and they took her."

"They, you mean the Serbs?"

"Yes, the Chetnicks," Mira confirmed, not raising her eyes from the papers. "They raped thousands of Moslem women."

Rape. The smell of hay in that hayloft of long ago came back instantly, the animals' tramping below. Thirty-five years ago, Loyzi, the son of our peasant caretakers, had pushed me down, held me on prickly straw, his flesh tearing me open. The communists had redistributed the land and given most of it to peasants. My grandpa was allowed to keep only the house and eight acres. I spent one summer at the house and the peasants — now the landowners — taunted me. "Little mistress," they called me, and when I told Loyzi's father what his son had done, he leered. Now beautiful Emina and her daughters had become victims of rape, that oldest and most primitive revenge.

I took off my glasses and pulled my hand over my face to wipe off the awful picture. This meeting wasn't about me. I turned to Suleima and gently asked questions about her life.

"Where are you from?"

"Tuzla," came the answer.

"Do you have any family?"

She shook her head. She looked at her lap and her hands began plucking at the frayed hem of her tee shirt. After a while, she began talking.

"My father was killed by them. Shot in front of the house. His brothers, too. Then they drove us away like animals, herded us into buses and took us to the camp."

She stopped and aimed her burning eyes at me. She beat her belly with fists, tears streaming down her cheeks; I resisted putting my arms around her. A few people in the cafe turned; some left.

"We'd better take her back," said Mira, finally looking up from her papers.

"No," screamed the girl and ran down the stairs, but we soon caught up with her. Mira grabbed her by the arm.

"You do here what we tell you," she hissed.

"Let's go for a walk," I suggested. "It'll help us all calm down."

"Yes, so you can get a few juicy tidbits for your magazine," Mira turned on me, her fingers like a vise on Suleima's arm. "I know how American journalists work."

I felt that wasn't called for and opened my mouth for a sharp comeback, but said instead, "Let's sit down on a bench on Zrinjevac. Look at the trees."

Mira suddenly relented and nodded, taking Suleima's hand. I led the way and we sat down under a bronze-leafed maple tree. Mira lit a cigarette and offered me one, but I shook my head. I had kicked the habit a long time ago. Suleima looked around, her flushed face turning pale. She even smiled and pointed at a small black bird with an orange beak and said, "Look, *kos*. Probably doesn't sing here." Blackbirds were East European nightingales.

Mira breathed deeply, then turned to me and touched my hand. "Sorry Veronica. I'm just tired."

"So let's sit here and rest." The fountain burbled and even the street noises receded.

"Remember Vlado?" I turned to Mira. "He took off his clothes and dove into the pond in front of the theatre, and when the police pulled him out and took him to jail, he told them he was a philosopher. An existentialist."

Mira looked away and said in a low voice, "We were all existentialists. What a crock."

I was startled but didn't press the point. Instead, I asked, "What happened to him?"

She looked at me, but quickly looked away and said in a hollow voice, "He was killed in Lika last year."

Mira's reaction surprised me. I realized she had carried the torch for him all these years.

She collected herself and looked at me, her eyes bright. "He drew up the Croatian resolution of separation in 1990."

What was there to say? After a while we stood up, and jostling people who crowded the narrow sidewalk, wandered west on Masaryk Street. We looked at posters and store windows while I snapped pictures. Even Suleima let me take a few shots. Stores displayed current fashions, and we stopped in front of a shoe store featuring square looking stacked shoes. Suleima pointed at a particularly clunky pair and burst out laughing.

"Our imitation of Italian fashions," sighed Mira. She wore flats, Suleima pretty leather slippers.

I put my hand on Suleima's shoulder, small as a sparrow's and equally bony. "Look at those pretty smocks over there." I pointed to the next window, a maternity shop with a number of hand-embroidered smocks in the window. I felt Suleima shudder under my hand, but I gave her a gentle squeeze. She turned to me, eyes wide. "That blue one is really pretty." She pointed at a blue smock with eyelet appliqué and a cross-stitch pattern in dark blue and red.

"Traditional patterns," Mira said. "Copied from peasant dresses."

"Come on." I took Suleima by hand and pushed open the narrow door. A bell tinkled and a woman rose from a chair behind the counter, her face a picture of disdain and her thin hair a flaming wreath.

"What would you like?" the crone asked brusquely.

I pointed at the smock, and Suleima reached for it.

"Keep your dirty hands off, you trash," the woman barked. Suleima

49

recoiled and turned to the door.

"Do you want to make a sale or not?" I asked.

The woman shrugged and sat down. I reached for the smock and held it against Suleima's small figure.

"A bit big, isn't it?" said Mira.

"She'll expand," I countered, remembering my own figure when I carried Ivan. "Later she can wear it as an all-purpose smock."

Mira shrugged. "Typically American."

Suleima was smiling broadly. I paid for the smock an exorbitant price of 125 kuna, 25 dollars. When Mira protested, I told her that the girl's happy face was worth every penny. Outside I asked Mira why the woman was so rude to us.

"Our people still don't realize you have to be polite if you want to sell anything. They think they're doing you a favor."

Suleima slipped on the smock. "Mama used to wear pretty smocks like this one. She was so beautiful," she said wistfully. Abruptly she threw her skinny arms around my neck and burst into tears. Enormous tenderness flooded me. That other baby that I had lost would be Suleima's age now. Maybe a girl, too, wearing pretty smocks. So I hugged Suleima and helped her cry.

When Suleima pulled away, I handed her a piece of tissue to blow her nose. Mira chewed her nails and glared. I looked around, suddenly embarrassed, but nobody was paying attention. A group of old women dressed in black stood in the middle of the street, shouting at one another.

"You know, my mother used to live somewhere around here," Suleima broke the silence, sniffling. "We used to visit grandma and grandpa before they died."

I exchanged looks with Mira. "Your mother? What was her name before she got married?" I asked.

Mira and I held breath until she answered, "Emina Hadzhibegovich."

"You know what, Suleima," exclaimed Mira. "Veronica and I went to school with your mother. Emina was the most beautiful girl in class."

Suleima nodded, her sharp little face crumpling, but she held back her tears. "I still have pictures of her," I said as we wound our way uptown to the school, which opened on our first ring. A small-faced nun with a long nose grabbed Suleima's hand and shook her.

"You've been gone too long," she scolded Mira in a shrill voice. She pulled the black head cover forward and her bony fingers tucked loose strands of gray hair under. Suleima's eyes glazed and she looked at me beseechingly.

"May I take her out again?" I asked. "Tomorrow?"

The nun nodded. "But make sure you bring her back on time. We don't want these girls running around."

***

On our way down the cobbled streets of the Uptown, I wondered aloud, "What'll happen to her? To the baby? Can she have an abortion?"

Mira answered curtly, "As you see the nuns have taken her in. No abortion."

"But they can't make her carry the baby. That's barbaric."

"She's alive and will get government help," Mira answered in a flat voice. "We have very good psychiatrists."

"Mira, what happened to the compassion that led you to medicine?"

"I can't afford compassion."

The discouragement and irony in her voice gave way to hysteria. "We have fought for all this too hard. Sacrificed for freedom and independence and..."

"What happened to the fight for that other freedom?" I interrupted impatiently, but Mira wasn't listening. Her eyes wide open, she seemed to be listening to the wounded voice within. Later I would try to tell her about that true freedom that goes beyond nationalist wars. The sixties had touched us here too.

"You're a Croat, too," she turned on me fiercely.

"Am I?" I mumbled, thinking maybe I was just an American. Suddenly I longed for America, the universal Noah's Ark, where nationalism dissipated or sublimated into ethnic food and dances.

"You ought to understand," Mira shouted.

"I do," I took her arm and suggested we go to the Hotel Esplanade, have a drink, maybe watch a movie. We both needed a break, but she shook me off.

"How many hours a week do you work?" I asked her.

"Sixty or... I don't know."

"See, you need a rest. Besides, I'm here. I'll help you get aid for the refugees. I can, you know. But now you must come with me."

We passed the statue of Governor Jelachich, the old patriot still lording it over the Croats, his bronze horse freshly scrubbed.

"We put Scotch Guard on him," Mira pointed to the statue, her voice tinged with irony. "So pigeon shit won't stick to him."

She took my hand and we walked in silence, lost on an island of memories.

"Listen, Veronica," she finally said. "We'll have dinner at the hotel later and I'll spend the night, but I have to go to the hospital now. See you at seven, okay?"

She kissed me and pulled away, the new, crisp Mira again. Her back straight, she fought her way through the crowds, while I slowly returned to the hotel. I wondered what I was doing in the old country, changed by war into something I didn't recognize and where I didn't seem to belong.

***

Later at the hotel, the air perfumed, Mira and I took a bottle of Slivovitz to my room and turned on television. The plum brandy was first-rate, and an old comedy with Goldie Hawn was on. I hadn't seen Mira laugh so hard and so heartily since high-school days. She was wiping tears when she collapsed on the bed.

"See, you need to come and visit me in Seattle," I said. "We can have lots of laughs together."

"Oh, Veronica, I wish I could."

We sat on the bed for a while, quiet. Mira turned off the light on her side with a sigh. "Good night. I must get up early."

***

I still remember the dream as vividly as I did when I first awoke. I was floating over a field of flowers—mostly white daisies and purple clover—while clouds raced overhead as if pulled on a string. Some were white and fluffy, some dark, movie-quality clouds. Human beings floated by, their faces blurred. Then the landscape streamed by, everything moving faster and faster until I realized I was dead. But I knew I was dreaming and I was saying to myself, "I'm dreaming that I'm dead." Then the scenery suddenly stopped and became a backdrop like a theatrical prop, and I was dangling between the field and the clouds like a puppet.

"Where am I?" I shouted.

Only echoes answered, each coming from a different direction. A light breeze sprang up and blew me and the clouds back and forth. A moment later I was dropped onto the ground, and I started walking, but nothing had changed. Everything remained in place, as if blown by the breeze like banners.

Sweat poured down my back, and my heart pounded when I woke up. Next to me, Mira slept soundly, her left hand pillowing her cheek, a picture of peace. How I envied her. She knew who she was, where she belonged and what to do. A sense of total helplessness overwhelmed me, and I buried my head in my pillow. Poor Suleima, I found myself thinking, her little face tugging at me. All alone there in that damp moldy basement of that old school.

I turned on my back, hands under my head, and contemplated the baroque ceiling, the gilded edges flickering in the flashing light from outside. Little Cupids held bows and garlands as they bestowed beatific smiles on sleeping forms below.

Extend The Lease

Third Place Nonfiction

Though we weep your death
As we harken the angels call
That which we reaped from your life
Stands above all…
      Sadie, Gene, Dale

These simple but powerful words had been repeated by Sadie Willett so often during the past two weeks. They were now etched in her mind, just as they were on the plain copper urn that quietly, but powerfully, reposed behind the clear beveled brass framed door of the cubical built into the marble wall of the mausoleum.

Sitting with Sadie on a small tapestry stool facing the urn, I noticed a slight smile of sadness reflected in her eyes; really a smile, a fact many might think strange if they didn't know the Willetts.

Married for 44 years, the last 15 found Dubb and Sadie as close and inseparable as Siamese twins, one never out of sight, mind, or contact with the other.

They had shared everything: thoughts, feelings, Jack Daniels sipping, and even the bathtub.

Even now, I could sense that Sadie's thoughts were reaching Dubb, swirling around touching him over the vast expanse separating life and death. In one way, though, life and death are parted only by a thin veil, the veil of death. Yes, Sadie knew her beloved Dubb was at rest.

Dubb had been in this room before. He and Sadie had stood here before, not saying anything but, without a doubt, communicating. They had discussed cremation many times and were in complete agreement, notwithstanding the objections or casual hints of disapproval from the closest relatives.

But that was Dubb. His whole life was devoted to the outdoors. He abhorred the thought of being confined to a cold, dark, steely, death coffin shut off from the world by layers of sand, dirt, and rock.

Yes, he was happy now, relieved of the insidious, death-dealing, pain-killing cancer that had transported him through that thin veil. At rest at last behind the crystal-clear door facing a stained glass window warmed by the radiant sun. A beautiful place atop a cool manicured grassy knoll overlooking the San Antonio River.

I'm sure Sadie felt the same freedom and calm solace on the seat facing Dubb that she had enjoyed uncountable times when she shared the old weathered stump-seat in the deer blind on their lease with him. Sadie knew how Dubb lived for the freedom of the fresh desert air and warm sunrise, waiting patiently for the ever so slight movement of the deer, stepping through the brush. I know Sadie had speculated at the end of each hunting season for the past ten years whether each would be the final hunt. It was a joyous day each year when Sadie heard Dubb say, "Sadie Ruth, call and extend the lease."

It hardly seems possible. Time is so fleeting. When time is shared with those you love, you just want to reach out, grasp the hands and force them to a stop. Only now could Sadie roll back those hands and relive those times past. Time could not erase her memories. Fortunately she could recess the bad times in her mind but the good times remained etched as on a clay tablet, to be recovered from the depths, brought to the surface, and molded to drift and sway slowly for their radiant warmth.

Yes, only now was it possible for Sadie to just relax and remember. I could sense that she was remembering as her eyes blinked a perfect glistening tear to the white polished marble floor. Her eyes then closed tightly as if to block out everything except those memories she wanted to float softly into subconscious reality; sweet memories that could easily carry her till she too parted that veil. I too began to remember.

It was 3 August 1980 at 8:00 in the morning when the phone rang at my home in Niceville, Florida. Sadie, very calmly and matter-of-fact, said, "Dale, Dubb died a few minutes ago."

Sadie sensed my fumbling for words of comfort and condolence, and quickly and resolutely said, "It's okay. Dubb is at rest. His suffering is over, and my heart and spirits are lifted." That was Sadie, always a real trooper.

A pint-sized woman of four feet twelve inches with unequaled strength, determination, and resolve, she was the glue that had held our family together for so many years.

She was the one who provided direction, caution, meaning, and sensibleness to the three "men" in her life, all of who were oft-times impatient, head-strong, sometimes directionless, and on too many occasions, entirely lacking any sense of caution.

Sadie's resolve was severely tested during her last ten years with Dubb, while she lock-stepped with him every inch, mile, and day of his battle with cancer. She was impervious, though, to any and all attacks. She never faltered, and practically did it alone, with very little help from my brother or me.

Looking back now, I wish I had known what Sadie and Dubb were fighting. I'm sure I could have visited more often. I could have called or written more often. A simple, "What can I do?" is the least I could have offered. But I didn't do anything. I didn't do anything because I didn't know anything.

When Dubb first discovered he had prostate cancer, I had just turned thirty and had received notification that I was being sent to Viet Nam. My entire focus was on my wife, my two-year old daughter, and the pending remote assignment to Viet Nam. I also had never known Dubb to have any medical problems of significance. He was always strong as a bull — I had never seen him with a common cold. The only pills he ever took were aspirin to combat a morning-after hangover. I don't guess "prostate cancer" made much of an impact on me. If it did, I probably just assumed it was something Dubb could handle without even trying. I just knew that Dubb would always be there, my entire life, fit as a fiddle.

I learned differently.

Dubb had many medical problems those last ten years. Sadie never told me that Dubb fell off the back of their camper and broke his leg. Or that he fell off his trail bike and broke his jaw and lost a number of teeth. Or that he sliced his hand open with a hunting knife and got a bad infection. He was castrated in an attempt to cut off the life-line to his prostate cancer and he fell and broke his hip. His prostate cancer spread to his brain and he was in constant pain from the chemo and cobalt treatments.

I learned about all of these things after Dubb's death.

When I asked Sadie why they never kept my brother and me abreast of what was going on, she explained that she and Dubb had discussed the topic extensively and both agreed "not to bother the boys." They felt that there was nothing we could do, so why bother us.

According to Sadie, "You and Gene had your own lives and your own problems."

Looking back now, I can't believe that I somehow didn't pick up on how things were going on the home front. I also can't imagine how Sadie was able to shoulder all of this pressure on her own. But I do understand. Dubb and Sadie would probably be considered outsiders by many. They were generally loners. They lived their lives for each other. They took care of each other. They kept their problems to themselves. They were totally dependent on each other, and I'm sure they took pride in the strength and endurance of their exclusiveness. They were so close and so dependent that they read each other as a single volume, intricately woven and bound by love, devotion, and understanding. The old saying, "their life was an open book" was certainly not apropos in their case. They were perfectly happy with the doors closed. They did not need nor did they seek the stimulation of outside contact. Together, they were a self-actualizing team.

Sitting With Mother

First Place Poetry

I survey the landscape of your illness
laid out like a banquet on your sick bed.
Chenille dots etch your face where pain has not.
Your name, a word I say for myself,
does not reach you in the sandflats of sleep,
where you pause in the new shade of a slash pine grove,
hang your name on a bird in the gallberry bushes.
You dance away from me
through gray-green clouds of deer moss
on new legs, strong with live oak bones.
I am tangled in your vacant house,
the growing grief of this failing day,
afraid with night you'll steal away
or turn to me, touch my face,
decide to stay.

Farewell

Honorable Mention Fiction

I notice them as I glance around the waiting room for a place to sit. They are standing in an awkward little group near the end of the rows of seats and look like something right out of a Norman Rockwell painting: a young soldier at the airport being sent off by his family and girlfriend. The only empty seat to be seen is right next to them, and I hesitate a moment before taking it. There are never any extra people in Rockwell paintings and I don't want to intrude on them.

I slip into the seat like someone easing into a pool of cold water, trying to not make a splash. The soldier's brother is closest to me, and I hear a thumping sound coming from the headset dangling around his neck. I surmise that he's not playing any of my favorite tunes. I give the girlfriend a passing glance.

These short skirts and tight skimpy blouses make it a challenge to glance and not ogle. She is a cute little thing — short skirt and there is no doubt in my mind that she is a girlfriend and not a sister — sisters don't stand that close. Her tattoos and the gold stud in her nose don't do much for me, and I wonder how Norman would have handled that — small butterfly above the ankle and a larger one toward the back of her thigh above the knee. It seems to beg the question, "Don't butterflies travel in threes?" Beauty and the beholder, I suppose. But he would have done a good job capturing the glisten of the tears in her eyes. Welcome to the real world, Darlin'.

Some parts of it just aren't all that much fun.

The star of this little tableau is a young guy wearing dress Army greens. He looks good in his uniform, but it doesn't seem to fit him quite right. He reminds me of a little boy whose mom bought him a suit to grow into. If he didn't have such a serious look on his face, he could be mistaken for a kid just playing soldier. I must be getting old.

Little brother, who is nearly as tall as the new soldier, reaches over and rubs the short haircut. "Are you going to let it grow out? Will they let you? Jeez, man, you look like such a doofus." He emphasizes the word doofus, but you can hear in his tone that it's lighthearted, maybe even with twinges of affection, not demeaning.

"Rick looks wonderful," mom and girlfriend reply, almost in unison.

"YOU are the doofus, Billy, if there ever was one!" girlfriend goes on. She apparently didn't hear any affection in Billy's tone.

"Good for you," I say to her in mental applause. Defend those you love even if you pick an unnecessary fight. That's what Tammy Wynette would do: "Stand By Your Man."

Her name is Trish. Trish. I suppose that's short for Patricia. Or it could be her actual name. Somehow, I don't expect someone with tattoos and jewelry in unusual places to have a normal name like Patricia. Something like Spike or Lucretia sounds more appropriate. I'm probably just jealous knowing that I'd never have the guts to have that done to me. Or maybe I'm sane.

Then out of the blue the opening refrain of "Splish Splash" comes to my mind.

"Splish splash I was takin' a bath
Long about a Saturday night.
Rub-a-dub, just relaxin' in the tub
Thinkin' everything was all right."
I wonder what made me think of that?

I wonder what Billy would say if I went over and asked him if he had *Splish Splash* by Bobby Darin? It makes me smile just imagining that.

Trish has both arms around Rick's arm and is clinging to him like a barnacle. Even the little girl who is beaming around like a crazed neutron — she must be about four years old — can't wriggle between them. She's a bad blend — an atomic-powered kid who knows she is cute and can get away with murder. I'm okay with little kids, especially when their parents aren't around. Then there isn't a power struggle going on. You can talk with them and they act like real people. This one could clearly benefit from a little more discipline than dire threats of "time out when we get home." I'm glad it's them and not me.

Rick bends down, picks her up with his free arm and says, "Are you going to be a good girl while I'm gone? Mama will tell me if you're not."

She nods her head in solemn assent and glances over to see if her mother heard. Since she has ruled the roost for four years, it's not too likely that she's going to become Tuesday's child now.

Nothing prepares us for these goodbyes. Not education, not experience. It's just one of those gates that we all have to go through. This scene has been acted out millions of times around the world: on piers, at train stations, airports, bus depots… at the front doors of farm houses, tenements, and mansions. The actors and the sets change, but it is the same story. The circle is being broken. We pretend that it isn't so, that things will be the same when we get back together, but in that part of us that is never spoken aloud, we know that life is never going to be the same after this day.

I feel for them and their awkwardness in speech, in posture, in feelings. They want to be invisible, but it feels as if they are on stage or perhaps more accurately, it probably feels like they are unwilling participants in game at the Coliseum. Is there a right way to do this? What are we supposed to be doing? There must be something that is the right thing to say:

"Give us a call when you get there."

"I'll tell Grandma that you send your love… she wanted to be here today."

"Can I use your shotgun?"

"Sissy is going to miss you, she cried and cried while you were in Basic."

"Will you write to me every day? I'll write to you every day."

I get lost in the melody of their monologues, and my heart goes back to the last time I sang this song. Good Lord, could it really have been 10 years ago? We had taken David to start his first year at college. It was only 700 miles away, but it might as well have been Siberia. It felt that far away. Mercifully, there were lots of logistics to take care of for most of the day, but then it came time to leave him. That might be even harder than taking someone to the airport. At least the plane is going to *leave* and you have to turn them loose. It absolves some of the responsibility of choice.

We are outside his dorm… his new home… and I need to move the car out of the loading zone. All of his stuff has been unloaded and carried up the thousand or so stairs to the third floor. At least it felt like a thousand stairs. Younger brother Dan offers to take the car to a parking lot. No matter that he doesn't have a license yet. Paula would probably let him do it if I weren't there. Someone else is waiting to pull in and abandon a child. No, that's not it. It's two returning students. Their car is so full that I'm surprised that there is room for the music that blares out when they open the doors. They are laughing, but I know that they are impatient for me to move. I give them a wave to acknowledge their presence, but their attitude seems so inappropriate… like laughter at a funeral. I know that's an irrational thought. Screw 'em anyway. They can wait.

I know David is eager for us to leave. He wants to start his life.

We start our own monologues.

"Call us as soon as your phone is hooked up. Just leave the number on the machine if we're not home."

"Hey, Man, you didn't take my new Frog Skins, did you?"

"Don't get so busy that you don't eat."

"We'll plan on coming down for parents' weekend."

"Here's a few extra bucks in case you run into something."

"Hey! How about me!?"

Someone has to be first. "Take care, Son," I say, stepping forward to put my arms around him. Profound parting statements aren't my strong suit. I hold him tight for a minute and he hugs me back.

"I love you, Son."

"I love you, too, Dad."

And then we step back.

Poor Dan doesn't know what to do. Neither does David. They solve the awkwardness by shaking hands while they punch each other in the shoulder and admonish each other to "be cool." Then Dan gets into the car and puts his Walkman on.

Smart move.

I know that Paula is having a tough time. This is our first-born. This is the being that forced us into some semblance of adulthood. This is the child who made her a mother. There is a bond between them deeper than my comprehension. I am very proud of him when he gives her a hug, and lets her hold him tightly. She then gives him a quick kiss and a bright smile, and we are away. He is standing at the entrance to the dorm and gives us a half wave when we pull away. We wave out the windows. It seems so sudden, so final.

Paula has tears rolling down her cheeks. I pat the empty space between us and she slides over next to me after the obligatory fights with the seat belts. I glance in the rear view mirror at Dan as she moves over and register his "there are some things children should not have to watch" look. Nevertheless, thanks to SONY corporation and Walkman technology, it is possible to have a private conversation.

"This is what we prepared him for, isn't it?" she says. "We want him to be independent and able to cope on his own in the world, don't we? I know this is right. I know this is good. But is sure hurts." Then she looks at me with concern and asks, "Are you okay?"

I half shrug and nod my head in answer. I don't have the emotional vocabulary to articulate my response. Then she looks at me and says, "It's just so hard to let go," and I hear her words almost like an echo. I know those words. I have heard those words before.

Wow. I haven't thought of that in years. Maybe never. It was the day I left home for the Academy. What a zoo. It was a Sunday. We went to church as usual, and they announced that I was leaving that day. I smile now, thinking how mortified I was, and then all the goodbyes and good lucks. It was painful.

We had lunch at home and my girlfriend was there. I remember my two younger brothers giving her a hard time about crying, until Mom gave them the mother look of death and they cooled it.

I went to get my gear from the bedroom I shared with my middle brother, Alan. He's two years younger than me. I knew that he was eager for me to be off to school. He told me so. It meant that he could have the room to himself. It didn't take me long to double check my gear against the list that had been sent. You don't need to take much with you to a military school.

I was about done when Dad came into the room and closed the door. I wish I could remember all of what he said. I know that I was listening, but the words are a blur in my memory. It was a "do your best but you can always come home" kind of talk, and I know that I was touched by what he said. And then he hugged me.

I can't remember him ever hugging me before that. I know that he did. There are lots of old baby pictures of me with Dad, and then later me and Alan with Dad, so I know that he did hug us. I just can't remember that ever happening once we got older. I guess that was just the way he was raised. I know that I thought it was an extraordinary event but I can't remember if I hugged him back. I hope I did.

Then, an even more extraordinary thing happened. My Dad cried. I had *never* seen him cry before. It never even occurred to me that he could cry. In those days, men weren't supposed to cry. The whole thing probably lasted less than 15 seconds. He made kind of a soft, anguished cry and sobbed five or six times — he was still hugging me — and then he stepped back and said, "I'm sorry, Son. It's just so hard to let go."

The very phrase Paula had said a few minutes ago.

A boarding announcement over the PA snaps me back into this decade and I glance around to see if I was staring at anybody while I was zoned out. Apparently not. The announcement seems to have galvanized this little farewell party into action, too. I really don't want to watch them. It seems indecent to intrude on their moment, even as an unobserved observer. I actually try to look elsewhere, to check my ticket and seating assignment again, to read a few more pages in my book, but I keep glancing back to them. I wonder if this is what it's like to be a voyeur?

Dad looks at Trish and says, "We'll wait for you at the car."

She answers with a small smile of gratitude and glances to Mom to make sure that she is okay with that. Nice. And when Dad steps forward to Rick, she has the presence of mind to release his arm.

I know the dilemma the father must be having. Do you hug this uniformed son? Do you shake his soldier hand? What the hell do you do? Rick solves the problem by hugging his Dad. I turn around in my seat, looking across the milling crowd to see if there is anybody I know. I don't want to hear and see what they actually say because I know what they should say and don't want them to spoil it.

I stay screwed around in my chair as long as I can, but when the risk of spinal deformation seems acute, I turn again to this little drama just in time to see Billy slap his hips as if drawing pistols, aim his fingers at Rick and say, "See ya, Dude." He turns and saunters toward the exit, putting the headphones back up to his ears.

Mom is now holding the squirming four-year-old, but as she steps toward Rick, the child settles down. Maybe she senses the emotion of the situation, or hears it in her Mom's voice when she is told, "Give Rick a kiss." I am convinced that there is a sub-atomic quality of sound in a mother's voice that warns a child at the DNA level that this is not a time to be antagonistic. She leans forward from her mother's arms and gives her brother a sweet little kiss on his mouth. I can see her face when she reaches her hand out and puts it on Rick's cheek and softly says, "Bye, bye Rick."

I know that she knows.

I glance away when the Mom hugs and kisses her son, but I can still hear her say,

"We love you, Honey. Be good."

"I love you, too, Mama."

"Mama." Normally, that would sound a little strange coming from somebody in uniform, but this time it sounds just right coming from the heart.

She moves into my averted view as she walks away. The little girl is looking back at Rick over her mother's shoulder. She gives a small wave as they turn the corner and disappear down the corridor. There is no doubt in my mind that the little girl is a monster, but I can't help liking her. Still, I sure didn't need this much emotional trauma.

Mercifully, a boarding announcement sends Rick and Trish to the gate, and I am spared further involvement in the pain of their parting. Since I hate sitting on planes any longer than necessary, I wait to board until the last minute. I watch the people line up and surrender their boarding passes before disappearing through the gate. Rick is one of them. He turns and nods a kiss to Trish before he disappears.

The usual final boarding announcement is made, warning of seats being given away, undue delays, missed connections, and other terrible consequences, so I amble over to the departure counter. I can see Trish at the window, looking out intently, with tears running down her cheeks. I didn't notice him approaching, but suddenly Rick's dad is there. I wonder if Rick has forgotten something, but he just puts an arm around Trish's shoulders. I can see he has tears in his eyes.

I hesitate before I go through the gate. No one is behind me. I want to do something for them, to let them know that it will be all right — not the same, but all right. But I can't really promise them that. There are tears in my eyes, too.

So Walt Whitman Wrote,
So Wrote I *

First Place Essay

Of him I love day and night, though it feels now like a distant memory or a dream, it is not a dream. He is dead. I was the last person to see him alive, and the only friend to see him dead. I know he is dead because I saw it; the face, the body of death that encased him in a shell, solid with rigor and empty of pulse. I don't have to rely on frail recollections because I have photographs of those mortal remains before they left his final mortal home; underexposed snapshots in grays and white; ashen pictures as if etched in smoke. I don't know which is more haunting, the image of his sunken temples, cheeks and eyes, or the paleness of the portrait as its subject lingers between two worlds, caught in halftones, disappearing; not quite present; not quite spent.

Of him I love day and night, his body was sent to some funeral home of his own choosing somewhere on the west side of town, and cremated; where a stranger addressed, labeled and mailed a cardboard box of ashes to Middletown, Rhode Island; where someone poured the fine cold dust into a metal urn and buried it beneath a February tombstone of which I have only seen a Polaroid.

I've never been to visit that place, I don't feel it is necessary. His father, who had died just six months earlier, lies beside him in an adjoining grave. The remains of a father and a son lying next to each other, keeping each other company beneath the lawn-covered earth that is sometimes strewn with a variegated autumn or a December New England snow. Only a gray marble marker stands over them now. There's no one living in Rhode Island to visit their graves except an occasional groundskeeper who briefly stops but never thinks about whose grass he clips or whose leaves he rakes away.

As the hearse drove away that silent Sunday morning I realized none of that would ever be important, because of him I love day and night, his burial place is not there, there in some other state, but it is everywhere; not beneath the photo-gray headstone and not beneath the tongue-tied and indifferent snow.

His burial place is everywhere he visited, everywhere he worked, everywhere he sat and left the handprint of his presence; and his resting place is here, with me. It is in the pink porcelain vase with embracing golden leaves wound round about its hips. It is in his embroidered initials on the pillow that lies comfortably on the chair in the den. It is with me where he sits peacefully on a shelf in the dining room, a casually-draped shawl made a hundred years ago by someone he never knew but bought by him because of its beauty, and now it is mine to tender and protect.

And he hangs silently on the wall, luminous in the sun, a perfect pewter beatific hand rising from the sleeve of Jesus. And he is in the watercolor of two lovers poised in time, cloaked in speckled splashes of painted leaves, looking forever young, forever stopped before a spired tomb where they are forever remembering. They are forever there in that moment, in that place, which is no place, which is every place, no matter where their frame is hung. For it is in all these things, and more, that he is. His burial place is there where I read and where I eat and where I sleep. Even if his ashes had been lost or spilled and distributed by the winds, I know that he is here with me, and I am satisfied.

*Inspired by Walt Whitman's poem "Of Him I Love Day and Night" first published in 1870-71.

A River Runs Deep

Second Place Non-fiction

As I traveled the rural Upper Peninsula of Michigan on a sunny Aug-ust Monday, many old-fashioned clotheslines were hung with colorful laun-dry on the traditional wash day. They reminded me that not all of life's old ways have succumbed to modern gadgets and faster methods.

The scene also brought back happy childhood memories of helping my mother put out our laundry, done in an old wringer washer, and of watch-ing my father tying his flies and wrapping his rods, an avid fly fisherman, he. Mother and I laughed and conversed as we did our work, but Daddy took his fly tying very seriously, and he thought it "man's work." As I watched him, we sat in what seemed to me like a silent reverence that I never understood.

We traveled that August day to Grand Rapids, for the 32nd annual Fed-eration of Fly Fishers conclave, where we spent a week listening to, looking at, and learning the elements of what my husband and I envisioned to be the beginning of our new, shared hobby: fly fishing and its separate enti-ties. Being new to fly fishing, we felt this would be the place to best learn.

This auspicious gathering met along the Grand River, a broad, shallow flow of brownish-green waters that course their way through the metropo-lis of Grand Rapids. The Amway Grand Hotel and adjacent Exhibition Hall hosted the 140-plus vendors and daily free workshops given by the sport's heros and experts. A variety of workshops were sellouts and worth every dollar — bargain prices when compared to what these pros charge else-where.

I found it interesting that, in what still may seem to be a man's sport, there are several women who place with the best of the men. And the men attending were just as eager to learn from these women pros as I was, names like Rhea Topping, Dorothy Schramm, and the inimitable Joan Wulff.

Dorothy Schramm, one of my casting instructors, started me out from a rank beginner on the first day, to actually fishing the Muskegon River on my second day of flinging a fly. We began that day's workshop, co-instructed with Ann Miller, with a class on knot tying and line building, followed by basic river entomology; "reading the river," they called it. I learned to recognize what insects are living on that river, that day, stuff that would be necessary to select the proper fly for a successful day of fishing — that is, if success is measured by number or size of hookups.

I suspected that for me, a successful day on the river might have been just that, a wonderful day surrounded by changing panoramas of rocks, trees, and rills, of sharing the water with birds and bugs, and feeling the wind brush gently through my hair; all this before a fish is even spotted or hooked. The hookup was incidental; the outdoor experience was the event itself. My day on the river with Dorothy proved to be just such a memorable outdoor event.

Our class of five female beginners shoved our fishing equipment into Dorothy's van, arriving 45 minutes later at what seemed like the center of an isolated, hardwood forest, parking in a wide spot on the narrow dirt road. We would be fishing the tail waters of Croton Dam and I had expected, at least, to hear water as we approached. I saw no clue of a river, and I surely didn't hear any familiar movement of water.

"We're here," exclaimed the diminutive Dorothy, popping the latch on the van's rear door, and jumping out of the driver's seat. The rest of us following suit. In borrowed Simm's waders and felt-soled water boots, I joined in the dressing ritual as directed by our instructors, an exercise of awkward wriggling and careful pulling, trying to stretch the neoprene wet suits up and over our socks, leggings and short sleeved shirts. My waders came to just under my armpits, fastening securely with broad, over-the-shoulder straps. Onto that layer, we each quietly added a pocketed vest, filled with tools, tackle, insect repellent, sunscreen, bottled water and a snack. Finally, a brimmed hat and polarized sunglasses completed our appearance as properly attired, neophyte fishermen. We were ready. We were a sight!

There wasn't much small talk, none of us wanting to say something uncool or to display our varied levels of ignorance at this stage of the game. A small gaggle of Canada geese passed overhead, honking as they do when they fly. "Hah, hah," they honked — I swear, a sound that mocked our awkward preparations for water entrance.

"Now," bubbled Dorothy from under her well-seasoned fishing hat, "we head for the river." None of us dared to ask just how far that might be, not wanting to appear wimpy or less than enthusiastic. Rod in hand, carried butt first and horizontal to the well hidden, narrow, foot path, Dorothy led the parade into the shady forest, the rest of us dutifully and quietly following a rod's length behind each other. The walk meandered along level ground for the first four to five minutes, through beautifully dense maples, aspens and a low, lush ground cover, then steeply down to another level, about 25 feet below.

I pressed on without comment, silently wondering if bear inhabited the area; it seemed they might . . .

Finally, we stood at the edge of a fairly silent, but shallow and swift river. The mighty Muskegon lay ahead. Through the clear, tea-colored waters I could see a nice rocky bottom, though we had to traverse about three feet of gooey mud to reach the water. We broke the river's silence with the squishing and sucking sounds of the black muck against our wading boots. I wanted to scrunch up my face and blurt out a "yuck," but instead, stoically stepped through the stuff as manlike as I could. I was beginning a new venture that I knew I wouldn't forget anytime soon.

Standing in the stream, Dorothy reiterated a few basic casting techniques, demonstrating how and where to cast our lines, then provided additional tips on how to read the river and find the fish we were there to get (and release, of course).

My mind had reached the saturation point, knowing that until I began to apply some of the valued edification I'd already heard, any new data might just get lost in the overflow. Our instructors finally released us to different sections of the river, where we would begin the application of their tutelage.

The Muskegon's 400-foot width provided ample area to test the waters, and I shuffled off through the ankle-deep water for an area of riffles downstream a bit. My first attempts at casting came rather clumsily, but smoothed out with a few additional tries.

I was finally fly-casting!

As a child, I remembered sitting at the banks of swift rivers, watching my father deftly curl the fly over the line and onto the water, and I wondered now, why he hadn't made the effort to share his knowledge with me when he was alive. Maybe he thought I wasn't interested. Maybe I wasn't then, or maybe I failed to let him know.

Now, my own feet in the water, I flicked the line out about 30 feet, landing just above the irregular flow of the nearest riffle. Our instructions had been to let the fly float freely downstream, resembling the natural float of a real insect; a "dead float," Dorothy had called it, part of a large lexicon of new terminology attached to the sport.

"Great job," encouraged Dorothy from behind me. She and Ann worked with each of us individually, always making us feel as if we were somehow masters at this sport we had just begun.

When the fly stopped its free float, I stripped in my line to cast again, mending the line as instructed, watching the floating dry fly for any sign of a fish's response.

After ten minutes, I spotted another area that looked like a place any wary fish might hang out, a large rock with a deeper pool in its wake. I waded out toward the rock, still only ankle deep, but a bit surprised at the river's force against me, making it difficult to move my feet into the shallow, swift current.

Several more casts of varying quality floated to their intended spots with no success... Well, no strikes, anyway. I couldn't have been happier, though; I felt successful. I was fishing. Moreover, I was fly-fishing, and I was standing in the middle of a river to do it, something I had never done before. All my previous years of fishing had been from boats, banks or piers.

I smiled, thinking that my father might have been proud of me.

Naïvely, I gave no real thought to the river, except for a fleeting awareness of the strength and force of the river's flow. Its depth and bottom seemed to present no real challenge. We were told this river had a good gradient, which probably gave me a false sense of safety. In the sheer excitement of just being there, I thought of nothing but where and how to cast on this gorgeous piece of water.

A former fighter pilot, my husband relates stories of good pilots being downed or seriously endangered because of target fixation, that phenomenon in which one becomes so focused on the pursued quarry that the realities of the surrounding situation are ignored, sometimes with disastrous results.

That is just what happened to me about 45 minutes into my first fly-fishing affair.

From my dad, I learned that fish rest in deep pools, often at the edge of a bank in the river, and often under the overhanging branches of a tree. I spotted such an area at the far edge of the river, and downstream about 50 yards. Casting all the while, I worked my way over to that spot, working on my own now, as Dorothy had gone upstream to assist other students.

The water flowed faster and much deeper in the area I had selected, which is why it looked good, of course. A large maple tree extended over the bank, catching my hook on three casts, but I reveled in a little smugness at being able to retrieve my line, and to figure out that I could cast laterally, or with a sidearm fling, underneath the entangling branches, as I had remembered seeing my father doing on more narrow rivers, almost 50 years earlier.

In my smugness, and determination on presenting the fly to the deep pool and the fish I imagined might be resting there, I only scarcely noticed that I had waded from the shallow, gravel bed of the river into a quickly deepening and more sandy area, where the river's force and flow had increased significantly.

From somewhere else in my past, I understood the physics of increased flow, caused by the change of surface shape, whether it be from the flow of air over the curved surface of an airplane's wing, or the flow of water along a changing bottom surface. All that escaped me for the moment, because as I kept my eye on the action of my floating fly, there was a sudden swish over my bait; a fish had rolled on my fly! He hadn't swallowed it, and I stripped in the line without him, but he had shown himself and an interest in what I was offering.

I was hooked. Fly-fishing would be my sport! The sport was underway, and I wanted to finish it with the trophy. I must also admit that the competitive part of my inherited nature also wanted to be the first one to hook a fish that afternoon.

Creeping in a little closer to the pool with each cast, I continued to place the fly so it could float to the spot where my prey waited. Repeatedly, my fish rose on the tasteless fly. My lips were pursed in determination, my attention was focused even more acutely, and my breathing was shallow and tense.

With a startling splash, something propelled up from below the water in front of my face, nearly hitting my chin, and shocking me so that I nearly dropped my new rod. Thankfully, my reflexes are still quite good, and before I even recognized the propellant as the plastic tube of sunscreen from my vest pocket, I reached out and grabbed it midair with my left hand. And before I could be amazed at my own quickness, I realized that the vest pocket containing the tube was now completely immersed under the surface, the water flowing just above my waist, forcing the near-empty tube upwards.

In the same instant, I realized I had wandered well across the river into a deepening pool at the downstream edge of a steep drop off. At best, the stout currents that pushed hard against my whole lower torso now threatened to knock me off me feet; the worst also flashed across my mind in a moment of panic. I froze in place, but as quickly as the worst fears came I knew I'd have to overcome the scary thoughts they brought, focusing instead on how to reverse my situation.

I turned to walk back toward the shallows, but even the slightest turn threatened to reduce my already unsteady ability to stand against the fierce current. Still not wanting to lose track of the fish I'd been working, I poorly reasoned that the shortest route out of trouble would be into the steep upstream bank that led into the pool.

I tried pushing my right foot in the upstream direction, but I couldn't move into the flow; as it was, I could barely stand still against it. Instead, I carefully sidled a few steps sideways to a slightly higher elevation, and feeling a little more secure, proceeded on with my fishing. I felt doggedly determined to lure the wary fish from his hiding place.

Cast after cast, my fly appealed to the flashing fish, failing every time to embed in the creature. Mr. Fish and I were, however, acknowledging each other's presence. My complete engrossment in the challenging encounter with the elusive fish totally overcame the reality of my precarious situation, and I fished on, plastic tube safely stuffed down the front of my waders.

After 20 minutes more of encountering my hopeful catch, I faintly heard someone calling my name. Dorothy hollered something I couldn't hear, and I couldn't turn in the current to hear better. Still, she seemed insistent on getting her message to me, and another student relayed the word that the river seemed to be rising and Dorothy thought I should pull back to the other, more shallow side.

Reality washed over me with a chill, and I knew I had to take action without pause. It also meant the abandonment of the intense game I had going. I wondered if I could have made the hookup, given a little more time. I'd never know, if I had any sense about me, and I wanted to live to try the game again.

My first thought was to exit on the far side of the river, the side nearest me. That made no sense, of course, because I'd only be farther away, but it meant I wouldn't have to face the fast, deep water between me and the shore I came in from, especially if the river were rising as Dorothy suspected.

Knowing that there was no time to fret or fall completely apart — both serious options — I reeled in my line and approached the reality of saving myself. One tiny side step at a time, with my back to the ferocious flow, I slid into the deeper water, an area no wider, probably, than four feet, but seeming at the time like a mile wide and 20 feet deep. With my teeth clenched tight and my mind steeled against thinking anything but taking one positive footstep after another, I forged through the sandy depths and slowly worked my way up the sloping gravel shallows, fighting the waves of panic that wanted to grab me by the throat, sucking the life from me if it succeeded. The shallows came soon enough, but the depths had drained my strength for that day. Still, there would be other days.

I closed my eyes during the ride back to the hotel, reliving that first encounter with the river, flinging the fly with a firm backward stroke, returning the line forward with a quick snap, sending the almost weightless fly looping back over the line in a graceful U-shape movement, to the waiting prey below the surface.

What a wonderful, magical experience, surely one I would love to have shared with my father. I have a new understanding of his silent reverence regarding the sport, and I'm thankful that he left me his old, beat up wicker creel, and quite possibly his love of fly casting as well.

Seventh

Honorable Mention Fiction

Grandma Lueke was on her deathbed, and they said it was for real this time. Her whole family was gathering at her farm out in the backcountry, and she'd asked for me in particular, so I had to go. Sometimes I made myself scarce when Mama and Daddy were loading up the pickup for family reunions or one of Grandma's birthday celebrations. "Oh, you have to go, Justine. Grandma's old. This could be the last time you see her," my mama would say. 'Course, it never was, and Grandma kept adding birthdays like a tree trunk adds rings.

I knew I was special to Grandma for some reason. She always asked me to come spend a few weeks with her in the summer, and I usually did because it was so nice and quiet there with nothing but the clucking of chickens and a cow mooing now and then to let you know you didn't have the world all to yourself. I didn't feel lost in a bushel of brothers and sisters when I was alone with Grandma. I'd feel bad if she really died this time and I wasn't there.

But I sure hated those big family gatherings. I had always been treated a little different by my relations, like the way they whispered stuff about me when they thought I couldn't hear. I knew they were talking about me, though, and I always found some place to hide out and read or think while the place was crowded. Sometimes I'd try to imagine what it was about me they didn't like.

My hair was long and black and a little stringy when the heat made it stick in sweaty ropes to my head, and my cousin Beth said I looked like a witch and should cut it short like hers. Daddy liked it long, though, and so did I, so I left it alone. I didn't really think that was a good reason not to like somebody, anyway.

Family gathering or not, I had to go see Grandma this time; Mama special warned me not to wander off before they loaded everybody up in the truck. At 14, I was second oldest of the kids still living at home, so my older brother Josh got to ride in the cab with my folks and the baby. I stayed in back and made sure the littler ones didn't fall out while we were bouncing over the ruts in the road. We had a couple of fold-out chairs back there, but you'd have to be turkey-brained to try to sit on one while the truck is on the back roads. And of course Grandma's place was on nothing *but* back roads, so the chairs stayed folded and we all sat on the bed of the pickup cross-legged and hanging onto the sides — Daddy wouldn't let us sit on the wheel wells — trying to brace ourselves against jarring our tail-bones too much.

Coming around a bend at the top of Lueke's Hill, I could see Grandma's farm sprawled out below us. It wasn't really a farm anymore, not since Grandpa passed away many years ago. It was just a little white house with a tin roof and a leaky cellar, located near the floodiest part of the mucky Winondot River. But she did have a chicken coop, an old milk cow, two mean old sows, and a little vegetable garden. And nobody in the family was about to tell her she couldn't really consider that ol' place a farm, just like nobody was about to tell her they'd rather have family reunions some-place that didn't smell like earthworms and dead fish after a hard rain, and didn't have so danged many mosquitoes.

By the time we were pulling up to the old place, there were trucks parked beneath just about every available shade tree, and Mama's brother Herman cut Daddy off in a spray of dirt and gravel as he raced for the last shady spot. Daddy just laughed as he pulled into another spot and said Herman was welcome to that spot 'cause it would be in the sun by the time we left, while his own truck would be cooling in the shade that would move over to cover it later in the afternoon. Daddy was pretty smart; he'd gone to school a lot longer than most of Mama's family had, but he never acted snooty about it.

Grandma had a big family: six sons and five daughters, of which Mama was the youngest. All of Grandma's kids had pretty big families too, so the place was 'tic thick' with aunts, uncles, cousins, and second cousins, and even a few old coon hounds that got dragged along by their owners to almost every family gathering for some reason. Guess some of 'em was more proud of their dogs than their own kids.

Such a crowd meant I could probably sneak off to the corn shed without being missed, sliding down the pile of dried, shucked hog corn through the window where it was poured after a harvest. It was a good place to hide out, because I had spread it around amongst the younger cousins that the rats in there were big as cats, and the snakes liked to eat the rats, so they were even bigger: nobody ever came in and bothered me. I would scoop out a body-shaped spot and watch the specs of dust appear and disappear as they passed through the sunlight filtering in through the gaps in the wood planks that made up the walls of the shed.

Unfortunately, I didn't make my escape fast enough this time because Crazy Aunt Dora was pushing through the crowd toward us. Of all the family members that seemed to dislike me, she was the worst. Sometimes when I passed by her she did something with her fingers twisted all funny around her lips to ward off evil, and she'd kinda spit at me. She had one o' them lazy eyes that peered off in another direction when she was looking at you, so you couldn't really tell if she was looking at *you* or the person standing beside you, and it was a long time before I knew it was *me* she was calling evil under her breath, and *me* she worried about getting cursed by. I started calling her Crazy Aunt Dora and it stuck with all the cousins since she didn't have no husband or kids of her own to stand up for her, probably on account of she had an ugly disposition that couldn't be ignored even if her face could.

When she reached us, she puffed herself up all important-like and said to my mama, "It's about time you got here! Poor ol' Mama's just barely holding on, waiting to see that little girl of yours. Why her, I don't know. But I don't aim to be the one to ignore a death wish." She didn't look directly at me as she said this, or maybe she did and I just couldn't tell because of her one lazy eye looking off at somebody else. But Mama knew who she was talking about, and she guided me toward the house. "She's laid up in the root cellar," hollered Dora after us. "Said it was cooler down there for laying a body out, and why have to move her after she's dead if she could walk on down there by herself beforehand?"

Grandma's logic never held no room for what was considered proper. If there had been an old lady-sized hole six foot deep nearby, she would've probably received her callers there, to spare someone having to move her body once she was gone from it.

People moved out of our way as we headed toward the side of the house where the root cellar stairs were located. The doors were laid open to let some sunlight in, so it wasn't hard for Mama and me to pick our way down the creaky old stairs, into the dank cellar below. The place had an earthy smell, like a freshly-dug grave. I could also smell other things, rooty things and lantern oil, mildewed quilts and moldy bedding, and something I didn't recognize. Death, maybe, but it didn't have a smell that I could feel on my tongue like the other odors. Instead it kind of rattled and whispered in my head like something was wading through dried cornhusks. Mama had taken my hand when we started down the steps, and now I squeezed hers to let myself know she was still with me. She gave mine a little squeeze back.

There was an old iron-framed bed down there, rusted but sturdy still, now that it'd been put back together for Grandma's deathbed. I could pick out her bony frame poking through the worn quilts that covered her from her twisted old toes to her fuzzy, quivering chin. Her eyes were almost shut, and if it wasn't for the tiny lantern flames reflected in those black slits, I wouldn't have known she was looking at me. I couldn't even believe this was the same Grandma that used to let me stay in the kitchen with her after she'd chased the other kids outside to play. That Grandma had eyes that were alive and happy, and could look into your heart to see when you were feeling down about the mean things others said about you. And that Grandma had a big smile that was pretty even if the teeth weren't, because you knew the smile was real and not about to be followed by something spiteful. I knew that old Grandma, but this one looked different, and I was a little scared of her.

Mama pushed me towards the bed, and kept nudging until I was close enough to hear the rasping whisper coming from Grandma's wrinkled lips, but not close enough to make out what she was saying. I bent over real close, and a frail-looking hand shot out from the edge of the cover and locked around my wrist. It startled me near to death and I tried to yank away out of pure instinct, but that old lady had me in a grip I wouldn't't've counted on from someone who looked like she'd break if you breathed on her a little harsh. The fingers reminded me of the chicken claws she used to always fry up and give to the little ones to keep them quiet while meals were being fixed. I'd gnawed my share of gristle off them little joints when I was younger, but the sight of that grizzled old hand with its paper-thin scaly skin and chipped yellow nails wrapped around my wrist would probably put me off fried chicken feet forever.

"You have the seventh," she said, strong enough for me to hear it above the whooshing sound of the blood rushing past my eardrums. "I have it, too. Makes us special, Justine." She nodded and squeezed my arm like I should know what she was talking about, but I didn't. I looked at Mama, and she just shook her head sadly and shrugged like she didn't know what Grandma was talking about either, but I should just play along like I understood.

I put my free hand on Grandma's and patted it and leaned closer, and her grip loosened a bit. "Come back later," she whispered into my ear before taking another quavering breath and adding, "Secret." Then she gave my wrist a final squeeze before releasing it and letting her hand fall so that it was hanging limp over the edge of the bed. I picked it up and put it back under the covers. She was breathing pretty steady now, and Mama approached the bed, placed her palm on Grandma's forehead and bent to give her a light kiss on one bony cheekbone. I left her alone with Grandma and went on back up the stairs.

For the next hour, Grandma's other children took turns quietly going down the cellar stairs and saying their last goodbyes. Lots of red, puffy eyes came back up those stairs and the talk outside wasn't loud and happy like it usually was. Other than me, only the older grandchildren went down to see her. Aunt Dora, who was bossy as a brood hen when it came to her ma's care, set herself up at the top of those rickety steps and oversaw the comings and goings of the rest of the family.

Like any other family get-together, whether it be for happy reason or sad, everybody had brought food along, and long folding tables were set up under big shade trees in the back yard to accommodate the bounty. Uncle Jonathan, who was a deacon at Jesus King of the Mountain Holy Church in Milltown, led the crowd in saying grace and offering up a prayer for Grandma's health or at least the peaceful repose of her soul, and then everybody ate.

I got my chance to sneak away to the corn shed like I planned, and I spent the alone time thinking about Grandma, and what it was she wanted me to come back for. I loved my Grandma a lot, but sometimes I admit I didn't understand her. I lay there half buried in the warm, dry corn, sifting kernels through my cupped hands, and remembered some of the talks me and Grandma had had on muggy summer nights sitting and swaying softly in the porch swing. I'd be almost asleep sometimes with my head on a flat, feather-filled patchwork pillow on her lap, and she'd be stroking my hair and telling me about how she could see things in the full moon. Not normal things we all see, like shapes out of the gray spots. No, she saw things like how far the river would make it up to her house when it flooded that year, and whether my cousin Judy would have a boy or a girl baby. I don't think I ever remembered to pay attention if the things she said came true. Somehow I just knew they would. She said she always knew which babies would be which, and when they'd be born, but she didn't always tell the truth about it, because it made people afraid of you if you were right too much.

Once she told me that I could see things, too, if I just knew how to recognize them. She said that one time when I was about three years old, I woke up from a nap curled up next to my two-year-old cousin Andy. Grandma said I was crying and I kept saying that Andy was in the water, help him, help him. I was soon quieted down with a purple Dum Dum sucker to calm my tears.

A couple of days later little Andy fell head first into a full water trough in his daddy's barnyard. He almost drowned before Uncle Joe noticed and pulled him out. Grandma said that Dora was the one to remember my "fit" the Sunday before and she had scrambled the story so much with every telling that she convinced herself and some of the others that I'd caused the accident somehow. When I asked Mama about it later, she said it didn't really happen quite that way, and that Grandma got things mixed up sometimes.

Grandma told me that story the last summer I spent with her before Aunt Dora gave up on living in Biggly, trying to find a husband, and moved back in with Grandma, saying it was because Grandma was getting old and needed caring for.

By late afternoon, people started to leave because the wind had picked up and the leaves on the trees were turning their silver sides up, which almost always meant a summer rainstorm was brewing. I came out of the shed when I started hearing a mixture of hearty goodbyes, vehicle doors slamming shut, and cars and pickups starting up.

Daddy had a tarp stowed under the seat in the cab, and he and Mama were busy getting my little brothers and sister settled in the back of the truck and covering them up with it in case it started pouring on the way home. Mama and Daddy went around and got in the cab when they thought everyone was settled, and I sneaked off and ducked low before they started the truck. My ten-year-old brother Seth saw me do it and looked ready to holler to Mama and Daddy that I was out of the truck. I shook my head and put my finger to my lips in a "shhh" gesture, and although Seth looked puzzled, he didn't say anything. I was scared one of my parents would look back and notice me outside the truck, but Daddy was busy fiddling with the windshield wiper and Mama was fussing with the baby. Squatting, I backed up and ducked behind the big tree we were parked beside. Seth hissed a loud whisper at me, "You're gonna get in big trouble, and I'm gonna laugh." And then he got back under the tarp and crawled back up to his place with the others. In a few minutes, Daddy put the truck in gear and my family drove away.

I climbed the tree then, and waited until the last of the family pickups were on their way. I watched as the line of trucks wound their way up the road and disappeared around a bend, and I thought the sight reminded me of a gypsy caravan except there weren't any horses, and the paint on most of the trucks was faded and rusted out instead of brightly colored like gypsy wagons were. Plus, my family just wasn't spirited and lively like gypsies that day. Then I thought maybe it reminded me more of an exodus, like in the Bible, and I wondered what the heck I thought I was doing going back in there.

Back at the old house, Aunt Dora was just coming up from the cellar. I heard her saying to Grandma, "I'll be back down soon as I finish some cleaning up here." She let the cellar doors fall closed with only a slight bang, and then I watched as she sat herself in a rocker on the front porch and proceeded to down a fruit jar full of dandelion wine about as quick as if it was water. I didn't have to wait long before I could hear her snoring in her chair.

The cellar door creaked a bit when I pulled it open, but not enough to wake up my aunt. I went down the steps carefully; there was only one lantern left lit now, and the room was mostly in shadows. Grandma looked to be sleeping still, so I sat down on an old, slatted rocker somebody had put near her bed, and I waited. I might have dozed off a little bit, but not much because I felt the tingly prickle on my scalp like you get when you feel somebody looking at you. When I raised my head and looked at my Grandma, she was smiling a half-toothless grin at me. I forced a smile back, hoping she'd get to telling me the secret soon so I could get back out of that dungeon and wait for Mama and Daddy to notice I wasn't in the pickup and come back for me.

Grandma's graveled voice struggled to be more than a ragged whisper as she started talking. "I'm tired, Justine. I'm so tired, but I have to tell you about something." She tried to clear her throat, then gave up and went on. "You know about the five senses ever'body has? Seeing, hearing and the like?" She closed her watery eyes for a minute like she was thinking real hard on what to say next, but I think she was just resting. "There's a sixth one that mostly just women have." She had a little coughing spell for a minute, then said, "It's called intuition." Her words were starting to come in gasping, breathy gulps, like speaking them was harder on her than lugging a 20-pound sack of potatoes up the cellar steps.

I waited for her to start again. After a minute she did, but her voice was getting softer. "Then there's a seventh that hardly anybody has. It comes and goes when it wants." Here, her head came off her pillows a bit and her eyes looked fierce as she said, "It ain't a curse. It's a gift." She fell back into the pillows and went on, weaker than ever, "I have the seventh, and so do you." It may have been the flickering lantern light, but it looked to me like her skin was sinking deeper around her sunken eyes and cheeks and withered lips. Then she whispered, "I'll show you."

Grandma brought her hands from under the covers and stretched them toward me. If spit were courage and feathers were fear, my mouth had dried up and filled with a fistful of goose down, and I couldn't swallow for fear of choking. But I gave her my hands, and she placed my palms against her temples and pressed them firmly there.

A current like a lightning bolt struck up my arms, and lights exploded behind my eyelids. I tried to pull away, but my mind didn't know how to make my body work, and then the lights in my head started to clear up and get closer and they weren't lights at all but pictures swirling around like a whirlpool. I knew right away that the pictures were my Grandma's thoughts, but it was some time before I realized the whirlpool was caused by the pain of dying and the medicine she was taking for it, and it was even longer before I could make sense of what I was seeing.

I kind of waded in with my mind and headed for just one picture. It seemed to help, because the whirlpool slowed down and soon I was just looking at one thing. It was Grandma, healthy and fleshy like she used to be, and she was sitting on her porch swing, swaying to and fro with a little push of her toes, just like I remember her doing with me. It was so real there that I could hear the crickets singing all around me in the twilight, and I could smell lilac on the breeze that was disturbing a wisp of silver hair that had come out of Grandma's tight bun. She smiled at me and held out her stout arms and I felt myself falling into them with no trace of fear left.

"You see," she said, "it ain't a scary thing to see in people's heads. You ain't lost, just taking a little trip." She'd placed that same old worn pillow from my memories of summer nights past in her lap and patted it with her hand, and I sat down on the swing beside her and settled my head on the pillow.

She started to stroke my hair as she continued to rock the swing and she talked to me about the things I could do with the seventh sense, how I could protect myself from finding out things best not known, how not to believe everything I saw in the moon or on a still pond or wherever the visions came, because sometimes they were warnings about things that could happen, but sometimes they turned out not to be anything at all. She said I'd learn the difference in time, and until then I should just be cautious.

She told me many things, and it seemed like hours passed, but at last she told me that it was time for her to go.

"Can't we stay like this for awhile longer? I don't want you to go." I was looking into her eyes and pleading, and I felt tears start down my imaginary face and a tightness in my unreal throat.

"Honey, it *is* nice here. But this ain't me anymore. I'm tired, and I'm ready to go." She smiled and wiped my face with her best lacy apron, and then she stood up and put her hands on the swing's chains to stop it from pitching me out. I wanted to grab onto her like a bratty child trying to get her way, and force her to sit back down with me. But I stood and we hugged, and then she turned and reached for the wooden screen door. I turned away, but I heard the long creak of its spring as it opened, and then the bang of wood hitting wood as it sprang shut.

The porch started to grow dim and small until I wasn't standing on it anymore, but watching it shrink and become part of that whirlpool I'd seen before. Then that was gone, too, and I found myself still sitting in the rocker beside Grandma's bed, holding her withered hands that didn't look so much like claws to me anymore, but the hands of someone old and frail who had loved me. I felt the tears still wet on my cheeks, and noticed that they'd been dripping onto our hands as we held them in our trance. I cried hard then, but not for Grandma, because I knew she was happy on her path. I cried for myself, because I'd miss her.

"Justine?" I heard Mama's voice from the top of the stairs. "Are you down there?"

"I'm here, Mama."

Daddy was up there, too, sounding a little gruff, but I couldn't make out what he was saying. Mama answered him. "No, hon. It's not the time for fussing. Wait by the truck, please? We'll be up in a minute."

Mama came down the stairs and I nearly knocked her over running into her arms. Through my sobs, I told her Grandma was dead, and she didn't ask what had happened, but held me while we both cried.

We stayed like that for a while, but finally Mama gave me one hard squeeze before she pulled away from me and walked over to Grandma. She put Grandma's hands back under the covers and pulled the quilt up to her chin, but not over her head. I was glad of that.

When we finally climbed back up those cellar steps, Aunt Dora flung herself at us, grabbing my arm and digging her nails into it. She looked like she was caught on the verge between blackest grief and darkest anger. But before she could say a spiteful word to me, I took her fat wrist with my free hand and stared hard into her one good eye, noticing for the first time that I was as tall as she was. I looked right into her head.

"Aunt Dora," I said with calm I didn't know I had, "you should give up on Mr. Vernskoetter. He's married, and he ain't gonna leave his wife for you, no matter what he tells you at night in the back seat of that big ol' Chevy." She let go of me like I was hot as a stoked stove, whipping her arm out of my grasp and backing up so quick she almost fell backward into the cellar. The picture I had in my head of my aunt acting like a teenager with a balding, pot-bellied thing like Harold Vernskoetter just about made me sick, but I ignored it and kept a steady gaze on my aunt. The fear of me that I saw in her face made me feel shame that twisted my stomach into a knot. I shouldn't have said it, but it was too late to take it back.

Mama was pushing me toward the truck, saying to wait there while she talked to her sister, but I stopped. "Wait a minute, Mama," I said as I turned back toward my aunt and spoke to her. "Before Grandma died, she told me she was glad she had you here to take care of her the last few years." It wasn't the truth, but I felt like I couldn't leave things the way they were.

Dora's chin shot up and the haughtiness came back to her face like it had never left. "Well, o' course," she said. "I'm the only one knew how to take care of her." She turned away and walked around to the front porch, dismissing me like I wasn't worth sparing the breath it took to say goodbye.

As we drove back up Lueke's Hill, bumping and jostling on the rough road, a tinny sounding country song playing on the dashboard radio, Mama said to Daddy, "I guess Dora'll stay on at the farm. Maybe she'll find a husband now, what with the land and a house of her own."

"Maybe," I said, even though she hadn't been talking to me, "but the house is gonna get washed away with the first spring flood next year."

Mama and Daddy looked at me with questions on their faces, but they didn't ask them. And they didn't mention my prediction again, even after the levee up at Bailey's fork broke that next spring, and the old house washed away when the muddy Winondot came up and pulled everything into its rushing brown depths, including Aunt Dora's dandelion wine and her hopes of ever living there with Harold Vernskoetter.

I don't know if what Grandma told me was true. I'm not even sure it happened. Maybe I just fell asleep beside her bed that night and dreamed the whole thing. And when the levee broke, I still didn't necessarily believe, since people had been saying that levee was due to go anytime. But I keep an open mind. And a closed mouth.

Miss Hilma

Third Place Poetry

Oh Miss Hilma, your well has run dry,
there is kudzu in your garden.
Hands, knotted live oak switches, strong,
snag the embroidered tablecloth
you smooth out around your coffee cup.
The washer on the back porch spins itself out.
You hear mockingbirds in the ligustrum,
the old man's tractor as it moves through waves of gravel
in a sea of pine and palmetto swamps.
The road snakes past your door, past fields of cabbages,
stops abruptly at the woods edge where the burned-out
shell of the berry-picker's house stands in ruin.
He comes to you resurrected by your longing,
crossing furrowed fields, winds his wedding watch.
You rise like the summer moon, warm coffee,
wait for him to fill the window above the sink.
The roar of the tractor, in a cloud of dust, arrives first.
As the air clears, he descends, hat in hand, an apparition.
Your cup is cool now, empty as a clam shell,
the gold long scrubbed from its rim.
You stop to smell the old man's shirt
in the ironed cotton of the tablecloth.
He is gone, leaving wind to turn a winter field,
and you, without a recipe to follow.

Melissa's Secret

Honorable Mention Children's Fiction

Bobby Puppy leaped in the air and ran in circles, trying to get Melissa Hen's attention.

"Let's play tag, Melissa," squeaked Bobby.

"Can't today, Bobby. I'm looking for a special place under these ginger bushes."

"Why?" asked Bobby. "What's under there? Is there buried treasure?"

"No," squawked Melissa, "but I need a special place for my secret. Go play, Bobby, so I can search." Bobby didn't understand, but Melissa looked so serious scratching in the dirt and cluck clucking, he knew it was a waste of time trying to get her to play.

Bobby was busy the rest of the day, running in circles chasing his puppy-dog tail and rolling in the grass with the other puppies, so he didn't think about Melissa. However, the next morning, he couldn't find her in any of the usual places. She wasn't digging for worms under the banana palms, or bathing in the little creek, or eating corn that fell from the horses' feed.

"Melissa, where are you?" called Bobby. "Do you have
time to play today?"

Wiggling under the ginger bushes, Bobby sniffed at a brown bush and jumped back, yelping. The bush had moved! "Bobby, be quiet."

"You can't talk," whispered Bobby. "You're a bush."

"I am not a bush. I am Melissa."

Bobby nudged the bush with his wet nose. "Melissa?
What are you doing?"

"I'm nesting," clucked Melissa.

Melissa was huddled in a ball with her brown feathers tucked in tightly all around her.

"Are you sick?" asked Bobby.

"No. I'm not sick. I'm nesting. Have patience, Bobby, and you'll learn my secret."

Melissa was acting strangely, but Bobby had a lot of playing and sniffing to do on such a sunny day. "See you later, Melissa. I don't want to stay under these ginger bushes all day," said Bobby, running off to find other playmates.

Every morning, Bobby found Melissa in the same place. She sat in a tight ball with her eyes half closed. Sometimes she sang softly. Bobby was tired of waiting to learn Melissa's secret. He complained to Bonnie Butterfly, who was flying among the brightly colored azaleas.

"I just don't understand. Melissa and I used to have such great fun. Now all she does is sit and tell me I must have patience to learn her secret."

Fluttering her beautiful wings, Bonnie spoke so quietly Bobby could barely hear her. "I had to have patience when I was a caterpillar."

Bobby stopped scratching his ear and stared at Bonnie. "You were a caterpillar?"

"Yes, a green caterpillar, but I worked hard, sewing myself into a sack called a cocoon. Then I patiently waited inside for a long time. When my sack cracked open, I flew away as a beautiful butterfly."

"That's it!" yelped Bobby. "Melissa is making a cocoon. When it cracks open, she will be a butterfly!"

Bobby romped away and scooted under the bushes. "Melissa, you're going to be a butterfly!"

"No, Bobby. I will always be a chicken," chuckled Melissa. "Have patience. You'll know my secret soon. Run on and play, so I can rest."

Bobby rambled off to see Tommy Bee. Tommy was busy collecting nectar from the flowers on an avocado tree, but he buzzed down to talk to Bobby. Tommy listened carefully to Bobby's story.

"I think Melissa's becoming a queen bee like my mother, Queen Beatrice," Tommy buzzed. "Queen Beatrice sits patiently in the beehive and watches the nectar turn to honey. Be patient, Bobby. It will take time for a chicken to learn to make honey."

Bobby ran as fast as he could and hurriedly scrambled under the bushes. "I know. I know the secret! You're turning into a queen bee!" shouted Bobby.

Melissa jumped at the noise Bobby made. "Bobby, do try to be quieter. A chicken is always a chicken, never a bee." Melissa sighed, "Please be patient. It won't be much longer."

"I want to know your secret, NOW," said Bobby. Crawling from the ginger bushes, Bobby laid on his tummy in the warm sunshine to think. He thought and thought. Maybe Ramona Robin could help me he thought.

Bobby found Ramona hopping around the flowerbeds looking for worms.

He explained what Melissa was doing and what Bonnie Butterfly and Tommy Bee had told him.

"Oh, how silly," chirped Ramona. "A chicken can't turn into a butterfly or a bee. Melissa is nesting."

"Yes. That's what she said!" said Bobby. "What's nesting?"

Ramona looked at Bobby with her sharp, black eyes. "I use a lot of patience to find my worms to eat. You will have to use your patience to learn Melissa's secret."

Bobby wailed, "I don't think puppies have patience."

"Is Melissa your friend, Bobby?" asked Ramona.

"She's a good friend," smiled Bobby.

"Then go and sit quietly beside Melissa, Bobby. With patience you'll be the first one in the yard to know her secret."

Crawling quietly through the tangled ginger bushes, Bobby sat close to Melissa.

"I will try very hard to have patience, Melissa," he whispered.

"You're a good friend, Bobby."

One day as Bobby quietly watched Melissa he heard cracking sounds. "Are you turning into a butterfly, Melissa?"

"No, Bobby. Lie still and watch."

Melissa's feathers started popping up and down like brown popcorn. "Are you becoming a queen bee, Melissa?"

"No, but something special is happening."

Frightened, Bobby jumped. "Melissa! Something is peeking from under your feathers!"

Suddenly Melissa stood up. She shook her feathers and stretched her legs. "Oh, it feels good to stand up," she cackled.

Bobby stared at the tiny, furry chicks popping up under Melissa.

"Baby chickens! That's your secret," exclaimed Bobby. "You made a nest for baby chickens. Look at the cracked eggshells!"

"I had to hide my eggs and wait patiently to keep them safe and warm," said Melissa, beaming.

Bobby and Melissa counted the peeping, little chicks as they popped out of their shells — one, two, three, four, five, six, seven, eight, nine, ten. "You have ten new baby chicks," said Bobby.

"What a wonderful secret, and I was the first to see them!"

Healing the Dolphins

Second Place Essay

The call went out to the Emerald Coast Wildlife Refuge volunteers — seven dolphins from a pod of stranded dolphins had been transported to our local Gulfarium, and help was needed to keep them alive. The dolphins had severe pneumonia and were desperately ill. Some theorized that the dolphins preferred death beached on the sand rather than drowning in the waters of the Gulf of Mexico. Sadly, disease was going to take a terrible toll.

The first night I went to the Gulfarium, there were only three dolphins left. The volunteers, veterinarians, and Gulfarium staff members were fighting to keep them alive.

Volunteers were expected to wear swimming suits and get in the water to help. Taking off my clothes in front of strangers would be uncomfortable for me, because I didn't like what the years had done to my body and didn't want anyone to see me. I decided I would wear my tee shirt and shorts into the water over my swimsuit. Maybe this would cover enough of my body so that no one would see my faults.

I arrived at the Quonset hut that covered the sea water pool called the 'tank'. The first thing I noticed was the heat. Large radiant gas heaters had been installed to keep the water and air warm, just as this species of rough-toothed dolphins required. The next thing I noticed was the noise made by the dolphins exhaling as they swam around the tank.

The tank was like a large swimming pool with a set of long wide steps in the shallow end. The dolphins were swimming in circles down in the deep end. Their loud puffs of breath were all that could be heard over the hissing of the gas heaters. The other volunteers were assembling for the nightly medication and feeding routine.

I stood at the edge of the pool watching the dolphins swim by me in lazy circles. They were so close that I could have reached out and touched their shiny, gray skin as they moved past me. They looked up at me seemingly as curious about me as I was about them. The dolphins communicated with each other using little chirps, clicks, and cries. I wished I could speak their language so I could chirp back at them. They seemed to be trying to tell me something important.

White numbers had been painted on their backs for easy identification. Another volunteer explained to me that dolphins #8 and #12 were females and #9 was a male.

It was time to get in the water. I looked around as the volunteers began to disrobe. They were all in swimsuits. I took my clothes off down to my shirt and shorts, but everyone's eyes were on the dolphins so I took those off, too, and just wore my swimsuit like everyone else. We headed for the stairs and entered the tank with the dolphins. The water was a little oily with a faintly fishy odor, but pleasantly warm.

The volunteers rounded up the dolphins from the deep end and brought them to the shallow end for us to hold. Three women, me included, placed our arms gently around the dolphin's body — we had #12, the smaller female — and held her for her injection of antibiotics and a tube feeding of nourishing cream and pureed fish.

Her body was warm and slick, and she trembled in my arms but she didn't thrash or try to escape. As large as she was — my arms just barely went round her body behind the dorsal fin — she could have easily pushed away from us and swum off. But she didn't. She remained passive in our arms as we murmured to her and held her softly so as not to bruise her delicate skin. We held this 8-foot long, 350-pound dolphin like a baby in its mother's arms.

She responded to the injection into the muscle of her back and to the large plastic tube that was guided down her throat for the feeding with quiet submission. It was almost as if she knew we were trying to help her. After her thirty-minute ordeal was over, we released her from our encircling arms, and only then did she swim away.

Holding female #8 was much the same, but I was becoming more certain the dolphins knew we were trying to help them. I asked a volunteer on the other side of #8's back if they had names for the dolphins. She said they didn't want to encourage making pets of them, as our goal was releasing them back into the wild. The less "taming" behaviors from the humans, the better off the dolphins would be. But I was already calling the smaller female Baby and the larger one Sissy in my mind; I decided not to mention this.

Each dolphin had an individual personality. They radiated emotions through their skin and in their cries and through their body language. They seemed to understand and co-operate and need us so very much. Even #9, the male, seemed appreciative.

I had named him Chipper. I got to hold Chipper many times after that night, and he got to know me so well that he could allow me to hold him by myself. Even though he was the largest and most difficult to catch of the group, he was the most docile at medication time. He quivered, trembled, and chirped frequently at first, but he was quiet after I placed my arms around him. He seemed comfortable there.

By the end of that first night, after I got out of the pool to rinse and dry off before heading home, I no longer cared what I looked like or what any volunteer thought of my wreck of a body. So what if I wasn't perfect? The dolphins didn't care or judge me or compare me to anyone else. They wanted me there — needed me there — to help them. Doing something good didn't require beauty, youth, or a slim body. It only required compassion, caring, and the courage to open yourself up to others. I had held dolphins in my arms and healed them and was going to set them free.

The two females, Sissy and Baby, were released into the gray dawn of early morning several months later. My Chipper wasn't with them. His cries had turned from cheerful to piteous, and the veterinarian couldn't allow him to suffer any more. He was euthanized to stop his pain. I wasn't there that night but came the next day and knew then that he was gone from my life.

But he is not completely gone. Sometimes I dream of him. We are swimming in the warm Gulf waters side by side. We are strong and healthy. We find Sissy and Baby and we chirp and squeak our pleasure to be together again. We swim into a river of moonlight glimmering on the black water and we never look back. We are free.

Wedding Morning

Second Place Fiction

The windows are rain-spotted, framed with yellow curtains that smile into limp Priscilla bows at the sides. The floor is waxed, but a closer look reveals traces of cereal embedded in the corner by the refrigerator.

The large refrigerator hums contentedly, belly always full, handle worn from repeated use, and paint thin from fingers sugaring across its surface. The eagle emblem on the upper right side of the door is now streaked from wiping with the loose-woven dishrag, crumbs and a purple thread sticking to the left-hand edge.

Her kitchen, where she is queen, is not pristine. Instead, there is a slight film of flour drifting across the countertop, pepper dots spilled along the edge of the sink, and yellow stains left by onion skins just to the side of the drain.

Cora is tall, dark in color. Her hair is tightly curled, close to her head. She smells of garlic and tomato sauce, the scents of nurturing. She scuffs across the room, wrapped in a chenille robe that ties around her waist. The belt that once was orange is now a soft metallic yellow. The sleeves are a little short, exposing her arms a full three inches above the wrist. The hemline is not quite even, shrunk from the dryer. Her feet are stuffed into crocheted booties with silver threads woven through. One still has the little fuzzy blue ball attached to the front.

She starts the coffee mechanically. Only when she counts the number of teaspoons does she seem to notice what her hands are doing.

Her hands are red, the knuckles swollen at the middle joints. Her nails are blunt with ragged cuticles. But today they are polished with clear lacquer. Her new beige Mother-of-the-Groom dress is hanging in the closet, ready for her to slip on. She must look her best today. She doesn't want to embarrass the boys.

Today. This is the last of the boys. Gone. She runs her fingers through the tight curls that never behave. The wedding is at one o'clock and he is still sleeping soundly. It's still early, only 6:30. She listens for the sound of his snores from down the hall. She walks to the window and stares out, seeing nothing. At least it's not raining.

The girl is so young. Christine is six years younger than Bobby. A short, apple-faced little thing. How can she take care of him? Will she make him happy? Fix him breakfast? Today young people just grab a slice of cold pizza or anything handy. Will she refuse him when he turns to her in the night, or reach out and hold him close?

Why couldn't they wait just a little longer, or maybe live here? There is plenty of room. Too much room. She could cook for them, help them out a little bit in the beginning. But of course, they want their own place. She remembers how it was when she and Ray started out.

She hadn't been much older than Christine. But she'd been much more mature. That's certain. Ready to settle down and take care of the man she loved. Raise his children. Take care of his home. Bury him with dignity.

Christine is a college student, studying psychology, for heaven's sake. Child psychology was the devil's tool. Look at the teenagers today. Mothers into theory and the kids into drugs. She'd never believed in that nonsense. She hopes when the time comes for the babies, Christine will abandon that silliness.

After all, her three boys had all turned out good.

Bill is an accountant at Harris's. Bill's wife Joanna is the looker of the bunch. Tall with short blond hair, really smart, she teaches school over at Jackson Elementary. Maybe that's why they don't seem in any hurry for babies, her being surrounded with kids all day. Cora's hinted about it to them, but they never act like they understand what she is really asking.

Benny owns his own landfill business. Benny's wife Marilyn is something else. She is into health food and that hoy... holy... holyistic something. And that long straight black hair, almost to her waist. She sprouts seeds, pays a fortune for free range eggs, and is so thin she looks like she would blow away in the wind. She's a painter, but isn't selling much. She does have some luck at the shows in the summer. Those "in the park" things that are so popular.

And now Bobby is leaving, too. He has a good little video store going, expanding into DVDs and games and stuff. No real money problems; he can afford that apartment on ninth street. But they could have a couple of the bedrooms here, if they wanted.

At least he and Christine hadn't tried living together before getting married. A lot of people did these days. That might not be a bad idea in some ways. Take the heat out of the decision. Maybe there'd be less divorce. But breaking up might be as tragic as if you were married. Maybe. Anyway, her boys didn't try it. They weren't brought up that way.

She pours herself a cup of coffee, sitting alone at the Formica table. She rubs her finger along one of the many scratches on the surface. How many meals had she served here? She wouldn't know how to count.

First she cooked just for the two of them, but it was really for Ray. She loved fixing his favorites, sometimes surprising him with a special chocolate dessert or a loaf of warm whole wheat bread. They bought this place right off, scrimping to make the payments. Then the children had started coming along. First Bill, then two years later, Benny. And in another three years, Bobby. Where had the years gone? The table full, then suddenly Ray was gone.

It was so unexpected, the heart attack. She never heard him complain, except about small stuff that didn't matter. Never about feeling bad. She guesses he really didn't feel bad until it happened, and then it was too late.

The boys were stunned, and it took all her strength to keep it together for them. She had a pension that was enough to see them through, though it didn't allow for a lot of extras. But money wasn't the thing, it was them sticking together, making it as a family. She might have worked at something, she doesn't know what, but she stayed at home, making things nice for them.

Maybe she'll fix pancakes. No. Maybe waffles. She wants to do something special this morning. This last morning. Who'd notice if breakfast wasn't ready tomorrow? Who'd care? What is the sense of this big old house with just one person rattling around in it?

She remembers when it was full of laughter and little boys scuffling. "Stop that, you're gonna break something. Go outside if you're gonna roughhouse!" Now they were all outside. Who would she take care of?

She swallows the rest of her coffee, opens the refrigerator door, and begins to search for eggs. Waffles. That would be breakfast. They were too much trouble to fix for one person, so she wouldn't be likely to fix them again anytime soon.

"Hey Mom," he said, stepping into the kitchen. "Umm, waffles?" He walks over to her, and wraps his arm around her thin shoulders.

"Good morning, Bobby," she answers, pouring the batter into the hot waffle iron. The phone rings before she can finish.

"Hey sweetheart," he murmurs into the receiver, walking with the phone into the other room.

After the waffle breakfast, the morning slips by too fast. She is showered and ready to dress when he knocks on her door. "Hey Mom, I'm leaving now. Benny and Marilyn will pick you up in about 30 minutes."

Can't he wait a minute more? She wants to hold him a second, say goodbye. Good luck. I love you. But he's gone. She'll see him at the church, at the reception, but that's not the same.

He's gone. Just like the others.

Gone to their new lives, new homes, and a whole world of new responsibilities. It's not that she doesn't want them to grow up and leave. She doesn't want to interfere in their lives. But it is too quiet already. She needs somebody to take care of. Somebody to cook for.

She thinks a minute, walking back into the kitchen. She opens the refrigerator, peering at the contents. She'll have to cook smaller portions or live on left-overs. She looks over the shelves, noticing ground beef still wrapped in its package. There are two tomatoes, four small onions and some grated mozzarella. Years of practice tells her how she can use it all.

Would Bill and Joanna like some lasagna? Maybe she could fix a pan for Monday. Maybe Joanna could stop by and pick it up on her way home from school. Save her some work, though Joanna was a good cook. She was bound to be tired after working all day. Maybe she'll ask Benny and his skinny wife Marilyn to supper Friday night. Heaven knows he could use a solid meal.

She goes back to look in the mirror, adjusting the collar of the beige crepe dress. She tightens the pearl earrings Ray gave her many years ago. Walking out to the front window, she looks, but they aren't there yet. She goes back to sit at the table to wait. At least it isn't raining.

Sycamore

Honorable Mention Poetry

The sycamore growing in the yard
near the street, when I was small,
cradled me, up high in liver-spotted arms,
girl thin, cool skinned.

I knew the larger sycamore
underground in darkness, aching
my secret self, beneath the lonely lawn,
sad little house.
I felt a secret world dark and rich.
Hungry roots hidden deep, pale as breasts,
thirsting for some sweet stream
sifted from long ago rain.

I wasn't there the year they took it down,
never heard the sound of saws.
I didn't see green leaves turning brown
clawing themselves into noisy heaps.
I didn't smell the wet green smell
as its rings and heart were opened,
exposed to the light of day.

I long for the shelter of its sweet shade,
my cheek against its skin,
and my mother, who once said,
"Oh what a wonderful tree."

Sons of Cuba
Novel Excerpt

Honorable Mention Fiction

Northeastern winds gusted off the Bay of Havana, blowing across *Avenida del Puerto*. Breakers splashed against the boulders scattered along the shoreline, releasing a soft salty spray. The massive bell tower of *Iglesia de San Francisco de Asìs* cast a shadow across the plaza onto the rainbow-colored canopies flapping in the breeze. The aroma of fresh fruits and vegetables mixed with the salty air.

Early morning shoppers strolled past the Fountain of Lions across the cobblestone plaza, stopping by their favorite *kioskos*, examining the produce and wares. The bell tower looming above exploded with a deafening cyclic ringing.

"*Se fue! Se fue!* He's gone," a boy yelled racing across the plaza on his bike. "Batista fled in the night. Cardena's on his way to Havana."

"Fernando, did you hear that?" Tangi asked.

"Hear what?" he said. "You can't hear a blasted thing over those damn clanging bells."

Tangi touched his shoulder, leaned over, speaking slowly in his ear. "Batista is gone. The rebel has won and is coming to Havana."

Fernando grunted, pushed her hand away. "It doesn't matter. They're all the same." He lifted another vegetable crate from the back of the rusty International pickup truck and set it down on the cobblestones next to the kiosk. He grabbed his back and winced. His threadbare clothes hung on his thin, frail frame.

"You've got to stop lifting," she said.

He ignored her, pulling the next crate off the truck bed.

"You're a stubborn man, Fernando Reyes. I don't know why I put up with you."

"You put up with me because I gave you a job and a place to live when you had nowhere else to go."

Tangi smiled and kissed his cheek. "You're right, I'm an ungrateful wench. I'd still be wandering the Cuban countryside if it weren't for you."

Fernando grinned. His weathered face and sad black eyes crinkled. He grabbed another crate and set it on the ground next to the others. "Get to work. You've got a customer waiting."

She picked up the vegetable crate and carried it into the produce stand. A young mother carrying a baby squeezed and smelled tomatoes. A snotty nosed second child clung to her leg.

"*Buenas dìas,*" the mother said, handing Tangi three tomatoes. "Please give me two of those onions, a couple plantains and that beautiful bunch of bananas. My son loves bananas." She ruffled his black curly head with her free hand and then wiped his nose on her skirt.

Tangi broke a banana off the stalk and peeled it for the little boy.

"*Gracias,*" the mother smiled, taking the banana from Tangi and handing it to her son. "Isn't it wonderful news that Batista has been defeated?"

Tangi took the selected vegetables from the mother and said nothing.

"The coward escaped in the dead of night for Santo Domingo. Señor Cardena will enter the city in a couple days. Isn't that exciting?" the mother said.

Tangi remained silent, smiled and finished bagging the produce.

The mother lowered her voice and leaned in toward her. "I understand the rebel is quite handsome. I hope I'll be able to see him up close. Maybe he'll kiss my son," she winked. "That would be such good luck."

Tangi watched the mother disappear into the growing swarm of people, somehow managing the package, carrying her baby and helping the other child with his banana. She smiled and whispered to herself, "Felipe, you've been victorious. Good for you."

She stroked her swollen belly; her love child moved. A deep lonesome sadness overwhelmed her; tears welled in her eyes. Maybe running away from home without telling her father where she was going had been stupid and irrational. But when she discovered she was pregnant, she couldn't face him, or Ramon Miguel.

What had she done? Why had she shared Felipe's bed? She'd ruined her life and everyone close to her for one night, one long night of sensual, unbridled, breath-taking passion. Even now, she shivered with pleasure remembering his touch, the closeness of their sweat-soaked bodies. She didn't love him, not the way she loved Ramon Miguel. Her body craved Felipe's power and mystique. No man would be able to pleasure her again in the same way.

The baby kicked. "You poor, poor child," she whispered. "You'll never know who your real father is. I don't even know. It doesn't matter. You and I have each other."

Fernando touched her shoulder. "Are you all right?"

Tangi wiped the single tear rolling down her cheek. "Of course, I'm all right, old man. You'd better get back to the farm and finish harvesting the winter crops. How are we supposed to make a living without fresh produce?"

Fernando climbed into the pickup. "Are you sure you'll be all right by yourself for a few days?"

Tangi smiled and nodded. "Of course. You just be careful with that bad back."

Fernando cranked the engine of the pickup. It coughed, and black smoke rolled out of the tail pipe. Tangi watched him pull out onto *Avenida del Puerto*, leaving her alone in the crowded, festive plaza with her secret and deep-seated sadness.

***

Tangi rolled over, opened her eyes, and listened. The silence from the street was a welcomed sign. For two long days and nights, she had stood at the window of her small one-bedroom apartment, watching the city of Havana erupting with chaotic confusion. Jovial crowds turned into mobs overturning and burning cars, and assaulting any known sympathizer of the Batista regime. She wouldn't return to the plaza and the kiosk until things calmed down.

She sat on the edge of the bed, ran her hands through her tangled hair. Would today be the day she could finally escape this forced confinement? She missed spending time in the open-air market, watching and talking with the people. Every day she didn't work, her meager wages dwindled, and the produce left at the kiosk spoiled.

Tangi switched on the radio, awaiting the frantic warnings of the newscasters to remain inside until civility returned to the city. Festive music flowed through the speaker. She turned the knob. No frantic announcers, just music and the daily farm and weather reports.

"Thank God," she said, heaving a sigh of relief. She snatched her clothes from the foot of the bed, quickly dressed, and hurried into the kitchen still buttoning her blouse. She grabbed a slice of stale bread and cheese, and then ventured outside the apartment.

The acrid smell of smoke hung in the air. The charred skeleton of an overturned car lay crisscross in the street. Rocks, bricks, broken glass, and other debris were scattered around the roadway and on the sidewalk. Tangi held the doorknob tight, resisting the urge to return to the comfort of the small apartment.

The door across the street opened. A buxom elderly woman, scarf tied around her kinky graying hair, stepped outside broom in hand.

Tangi crossed the street. "*Buenas dìas*, Elena. Do you think it's safe to return to the plaza?" she asked. "My vegetables are spoiling."

The woman leaned on her broom. "Throughout the years I've seen many leaders come and go." Her upper lip curled in disgust. "The chaos is over... for now. It's time to clean up and learn to tolerate the next bunch." She turned her back and began sweeping.

Tangi wanted to reach out and comfort her neighbor, convince Elena this was a good thing. Why was she so despondent? Fernando had also acted unemotional about Batista leaving and Felipe coming. Couldn't they both see the rebels represented a new hope for Cuba and its people? *They'll see. Everything will be better now... they'll see.*

She watched Elena sweeping the same spot, shrugged and headed for *Plaza de San Francisco*. The two-block walk to the kiosk revealed much the same destruction she had witnessed on her street, but the mood of the people walking about contradicted the devastation. Laughter had replaced the yelling, screaming, and sirens from the nights before. Everyone passing by smiled and waved; one woman even hugged her.

The bell tower of *Iglesia de San Franciso de Asìs* came into view. Music and singing drifted through the air from the plaza. Tangi walked past the Fountain of the Lions, stopped and laughed at two men dancing with one another. Half a dozen teenage boys jumped into the fountain, splashing water all over the pedestrians.

She smiled and wiped the water off her arm and face, resisting temptation to jump into the fountain with the boys. The contagious carnival atmosphere was fun, but she had work to do. Tangi looked back one more time at the silly scene and then headed for the kiosk.

The blue and yellow canopy covering the produce stall was ripped, dangling from the support frame. Wood from smashed crates was strewn across the cobblestones; trampled tomatoes, mashed bananas lay squashed on the ground; and cantaloupes and melons were scattered all around. Tangi knelt on the rough stones, gathering and salvaging what remained of the undamaged produce.

"He's here... he's here!" a woman screamed. Church bells throughout Havana began tolling, factory whistles blew and ship sirens sounded. The crowd rushed toward *Avenida del Puerto*.

Tangi, skirt filled with unspoiled produce, stood in the plaza next to the kiosk, watching hordes of people stream toward the roadway. She was tempted to join them, but a surge of apprehension glued her feet to the stones. Maybe it was best she didn't see him. What if he saw and recognized her? This day was too important to him. Why would he give her a second look, particularly now that he was about to become Cuba's new leader? She hesitated for a brief moment, and then dumped the mixture of fruits and vegetables into a nearby broken crate and raced off to join the celebrating crowd.

Jeeps belching smoke roared up the avenue. Rifle shots pierced the air above everyone's heads. The crowd cheered. Felipe, cigar clenched between his teeth, Yankee baseball cap on his head, stood tall in the slow-moving jeep, smiling and waving at the people. His olive-green fatigues were crisp and clean, and his semi-automatic rifle was slung over his shoulder. Seeing him from this distance still took her breath away. He had a way of consuming her, and it was best she forget him. Because of one night of indiscretion, she'd never be able to face her father or Ramon Miguel again.

The jeep carrying Felipe moved closer and stopped. Tangi stepped back deeper into the crowd. He got out of the vehicle and moved up and down the line, shaking hands, accepting congratulatory hugs from the people. He picked up a small black curly headed boy, and kissed him on both cheeks.

Tangi smiled, remembering the mother's wish two days earlier, and now it had come true.

He climbed back into the jeep. Their eyes met for a brief second. Tangi tucked her head; her mane of red hair fell across her face. She turned and walked away, fighting the overwhelming desire to turn around and call out to him — but she didn't. It was better this way.

***

Six months later

The Caribbean June sun bore down over Havana, leaving the air stagnant and oppressive. Morning shoppers had departed, leaving only a few tourists and stragglers wandering around *Plaza de San Francisco*. Tangi wiped her brow and glanced over at Fernando, napping in a nearby chair. A fly buzzed around his snowy hair as a soft snore escaped his lips. In an hour they would close the produce stand. She would return to the apartment for an afternoon *siesta*, and Fernando would head back to the farm.

Tangi shifted from one foot to the other, trying to find relief from the cobblestones digging into the bottom of her thin soles. She stretched her sore back and slipped off her shoes, seeking relief from the heat. The baby would be coming soon — too soon. The joy of birth escaped her, leaving only a deep anxiety and fear for the future.

"Get off your feet... Go home," Fernando said. "It's not good for you or the baby to stay in this heat."

"When did you wake up?"

Fernando got up from the chair and stretched. "What do you mean? I wasn't asleep. I've kept an eye on you."

"Don't spy on me," she said slipping her shoes back on. "I can take care of myself."

Fernando shouldered an empty wooden crate. "Somebody needs to take care of you. I would've never allowed a daughter of mine to get herself in this situation."

"Leave my father out of this. He doesn't even know."

He set the crate on its side. "I'm not blaming your father. I'm blaming the bastard who got you in this condition. Any man who'd not honor a woman after... after..."

Tears rolled down Tangi's sweat-soaked face. Fernando took her by the shoulders; his eyes softened. "If I were younger, I'd marry you myself."

Tangi managed a weak smile, touched his weathered face with the back of her hand. "You're not as tough as you act," she said.

"Not tough, huh? I tell you one thing, if I ever meet that sorry son-of-a-bitch who did this, I'll run him down with my truck."

"Fernando! You'd do no such thing."

"Excuse me," a man said from behind her. "Is this fruit fresh?"

Tangi whirled around, resisting the urge to lash out at the intrusion. She stopped, not believing her eyes. Every muscle tensed. She didn't know what to do... She didn't know what to say.

"Tangi... Tangi is that you?" the man asked.

Her heart raced; her throat tightened, choking her. *Nowhere to go, nowhere to hide.*

"I've been looking everywhere for you."

Fernando stepped in front of Tangi. "Who are you? What do you want? I don't like strangers talking to my daughter."

She leaned her head against Fernando's back, tugged on his shirt, and whispered, "It's all right. I know this man. He's from my village."

He jerked his head around. "Is this —"

"Never mind," she said. "You just go about your business."

Fernando backed away, keeping an ice-cold stare on the stranger.

Tangi tucked her head and spoke just above a whisper. "Yes, Ramon Miguel. It's me. How are you?"

"How are you?... How are you! Is that the only thing you have to say after leaving without any word of your whereabouts?"

Fernando dropped a loaded crate onto the cobblestones. Cantaloupes rolled across the ground. "Tangi, I'll run this pest off if you'd like," he said.

A flush colored her cheeks. She looked away from both Fernando and Ramon Miguel, saying nothing.

"How long have you been in Havana?" Ramon Miguel asked. "I must've passed through this marketplace a dozen times over the last two weeks, and not once did I think to look for you here." Elation, relief, confusion marked his face. "Can we go somewhere and talk?"

"I think you should just *go!*" Fernando said. "Can't you see you've upset her?"

Ramon Miguel stood his ground. "No. I need to talk to her." He lowered his voice, his eyes pleaded. "Please just go with me to that café on the corner," he pointed. "I won't keep you long, I promise."

A cold fear rushed through her. She was light-headed and nauseous. A pain stabbed her stomach; she winced. Tangi never dreamed this day would come, but it had, and now she would have to face the consequences of her pregnancy and running away. How would she explain? What would she say? It didn't matter. She owed Ramon Miguel some kind of explanation.

Fernando touched her shoulder. "You don't have to go with this man."

She took a deep breath and whispered. "I know… I know, but I must. Can you handle things here for a little while?"

He patted her hand. "Don't go far. I want to keep an eye on this one."

Ramon Miguel and Tangi walked across the cobblestone plaza in silence. She stopped and sat on the edge of the Fountain of the Lions. "Do you mind? she asked.

He sat down next to her and took her hand. She didn't resist. Tangi was too tired… tired of the running… tired of the lies. It was time for her to face her demons. There was something comforting about the trickling sound of water behind her and Ramon Miguel's fingers intertwined with hers — it felt natural and good. The first sea breeze of the day drifted across the plaza.

"I'd given up hope of ever finding you," Ramon Miguel said, squeezing her hand. "I've searched everywhere for you."

Tangi said nothing. Her throat constricted; it was going to be harder than she thought.

"My heart told me you were in Havana. I've been here for months, looking through the crowds in the streets, searching, hoping and praying I would once again see your beautiful face." He kissed her hand. "I've missed you beyond belief. When you disappeared, I wanted to die. Why did you leave?"

There it was, the question. Tangi stroked her stomach and forced herself to look Ramon Miguel in the eyes.

"Tell me you didn't leave because of the child you're carrying," he said. "You know I want children. I want many children!" He laughed, not waiting for an answer. "Tangi, Tangi, we knew this could happen. After all, we were never careful. How many times did I beg you to marry me?" He touched her swollen belly. "This was no reason to leave me, your father and our village."

Tears streamed down her cheeks. She had to tell him she'd been unfaithful and perhaps the child wasn't his, but the words stuck in her throat.

He wrapped his arms around her and whispered in her ear. "Tangi, my love, this is what your father would've wanted."

Would've. Tangi's heart skipped a beat. "What did you say?" She pushed away from him.

Ramon Miguel's mouth dropped open. "Oh, my God. You don't know."

"Know what?" Her heart pounded.

His arms reached for her, but she pushed them away.

"Just tell me."

"Your father is dead. He was murdered by the rebels."

Her screams reverberated in her ears. "No… No, it isn't true." Tangi beat his chest with her fist. "You're lying just to hurt me."

He grabbed her wrists and held them. "When you left, your father was frantic, and didn't understand why or where you'd gone. He went to the parish priest to ask if he knew where you were."

Tangi rocked back and forth in anguish.

"Father Camelo admitted you had come to the parish seeking guidance and that you had asked him to keep your secret. He told your father you were pregnant and it was your desire to leave so you wouldn't embarrass him. He also told him he advised you to stay and face your sin."

Tangi looked away. Ramon Miguel continued. "Lazaro blamed the rebels. He was convinced one of them raped you. I tried to explain to him the child was mine. He patted me on the back and told me how noble I was to try and make him feel better. He told me he knew in his heart you and I would never deceive him in that way."

A pain knifed through Tangi's stomach; she doubled up, grabbing her belly. Ramon jumped up to help her. She held up her hand, "I'm all right," she grimaced, "just continue."

"Please let me take you to a doctor," he pleaded.

"No Ramon, continue telling me. Everything. I need to know."

He sat back down on the fountain's edge. "The last time I saw Lazaro, he was heading to the rebel camp to demand they find and execute the rapist. When he didn't return home, we assumed he was still searching for you somewhere in Cuba. A few weeks later, the story of his death filtered down to the village." Ramon Miguel hesitated.

Tangi begged him with her eyes not to stop.

"We were told he stormed into the camp, dragging three rebel soldiers behind him, demanding to know who raped you. He insisted the guilty party be executed for violating his virgin daughter. The rebels denied that a soldier had done this. They insisted you had come and departed without incident. They dared to suggest to Lazaro you had a lover, or perhaps many lovers. These insinuations only infuriated him more, blinding him with hatred and loathing. We heard he lunged at the rebel leader with a knife, but before he reached Cardena, gun shots erupted, killing your father."

Tangi screamed; a final burst of unbearable pain ripped through her. She slumped onto the cobblestones in front of the Fountain of Lions, blood flowing from her loins.

***

"Papa, Papa, come back. Don't leave me! I'm sorry. Please forgive me."

"Shhh, Tangi, it's all right. I'm here. Fernando's here." Ramon Miguel said.

Her eyes flew open; she shot straight up in bed. "Papa? Where's Papa?" She grabbed Ramon's wrist, squeezing and digging her fingernails deep.

"Where am I? What happened?" Her eyes darted around the stark hospital ward. Empty beds framed by high windows lined the opposite wall. Darkness shrouded the large room except for the soft glow from a small lamp sitting on a metal nightstand next to her bed. Two white privacy screens separated her from the other patients.

Ramon Miguel kissed her cheek and laid her back against the pillows. "Everything's going to be fine. Just sleep."

Perspiration rolled off her forehead. "We were at the Plaza. I fainted-"

He dabbed her brow with a cool, damp cloth. "You've had a rough time. The baby is fine."

"Baby?"

He smiled, touched her cheek with the back of his hand. "Yes, yes, we have a beautiful, healthy son."

Tangi looked at Ramon Miguel, confusion furrowing her brow. She rubbed a hand across her belly, the huge mound no longer there. The baby was gone and Ramon Miguel was here. She had delivered the child and he thinks it's theirs. Guilt choked her; nausea churned her stomach.

She tucked her head deep into the folds of the pillow and squeezed her eyes shut. Maybe when she awakened from this nightmare she would be home in the *Sierra Maestra* with her Papa. Sleep evaded her, leaving only a deep sense of dread and hopelessness. This should be the happiest day of her life, but reality marred the occasion.

Ramon sat on the edge of the bed, took her hand and kissed it. "Would you like to see him?" he asked.

Words caught in Tangi's throat. Of course she needed to see the baby, but was she ready? Confusion, fear overwhelmed what should have been natural motherly instincts. Maybe later, but not now. My God, what was wrong with her? She stared at Ramon and still said nothing.

Ramon Miguel squeezed her hand, got up from the bed and disappeared into the shadows. She heard the echo of his retreating steps against the linoleum floor and then stopped. A cold silence was followed by soft whispers and footsteps returning.

Fernando peeked around the edge of the screen holding a small bundle wrapped in a blue blanket.

Tangi smiled when she saw the old man. His face beamed with joy.

"Look what I have," he said, laying the baby in Tangi's arms. "He's mighty handsome."

She looked at the small child in her arms. His tiny heart-shaped lips were pursed, cooing and making sucking noises. The baby had her father's eyes, and his head was covered with a wisp of pale red hair. The earlier dread and uncertainty engulfing her drifted away.

"He must be hungry," Fernando said.

"Oh my God, I don't know what to do. What should I do?"

"That's what those beautiful breasts are for," Ramon Miguel said coming around the corner of the bed. "Want me to find a nurse to help?"

Fernando glared at Ramon, his lip turned up in a snarl. "You're the reason the baby came early," he said. "You could've killed both Tangi and him."

She frowned, shook her head. "Please don't. Not now."

"We don't need him," Fernando said. "Send this son-of-a-bitch away. He's trouble."

Tangi shut her eyes and sighed. "Fernando, go find me a nurse."

"We'll manage just fine without him," he mumbled as he walked away. "You'll see."

She touched Ramon Miguel's hand. "Don't mind him. He's always a little bit angry about something. It's his nature."

"It's obvious he doesn't like me."

"He has a soft heart, a good heart, but doesn't trust any young men around me. He's just like my own father, overprotective." A pain ripped through her heart, and tears welled in her eyes — her Papa was dead.

Tangi hugged the baby a little closer. She was tired and wanted to be left alone. No Ramon Miguel, no Fernando, just, she and the baby.

"You can go now. We're fine. Thank you for getting us to the hospital."

"Go? Where would I go?" His eyes were wide in astonishment. "I've searched months for you, and I'm not letting you out of my sight again." He took Tangi's hand. "This boy needs a father. We both know I'm his father. Whether you like it or not, I plan to remain in both of your lives."

"But—"

"I'll never understand the reasons you left home, and I'll never question your decision to leave. All I ask is for you to allow me to love you as I always have. Allow me to be a part of your lives."

Tangi tilted her head to one side and looked at Ramon, her brow slightly furrowed. She had made her decision months ago: she would raise the baby

106

alone. But the complications in her life kept multiplying. She wasn't sure she could endure another minute of pain, another surprise.

Ramon Miguel said nothing. He just gazed at Tangi. His gentle brown eyes glistened with love and hope. Perhaps she and the baby needed him as much as he needed them. How could she refuse him? She smiled and switched the infant to her other arm, closer to Ramon. He sat on the edge of the bed and placed his hand on the baby's blanket. "What will you call him?" he asked.

"Andrès, after my grandfather. Papa always wanted me to name my first son after his father."

Celadon

Honorable Mention Poetry

— a translucent gray-green glaze
prized for centuries by master
potters of China and Japan —

It's the color
of sand and sea
where they confuse
at the shore

where the beryl fog
lifts hues from sand,
from plover bellies,
from sea oats
sprawled over dunes

from water-green veils
scrolling into shore,
from pulverized shells
bereft of color

from the surreal sun
unloosed from its way
and let drift as scrim,
visible as the light fuses

appearing same
but shifting from one
translucent hue
to another

dusting the
trickster dunes
with dew.

The Orphan

Honorable Mention Children's Fiction

I lived with Grandpa and Grandma over the store. It was called a general store because Grandpa sold everything from pickled pig's feet to ten-penny nails that were in wooden barrels way back of the store where the safe was, and the shovels and picks. I think Grandpa kept most of his money in the safe. Never heard him talk about going to the bank. And when he had to pay the drummers — Grandpa said drummers were salesmen — he always went to the big, black safe.

Sometimes Aunt Ada came to help Grandpa in the store. She always brought her three kids, Libby, my age, well, she was two months older, she kep' telling me, Dolly and Junior.

I was an orphan, and I never knew how an orphan was supposed to act or what was so different about an orphan. When customers came in the store, they often touched me on the head and shook their head at the same time, making me want to look in the mirror and see if something was wrong. But I never did. I just let it go because I figured orphans must look different than other people anyway.

I didn't feel any different except when I brought home lice and the itch from school.

Aunt Ada always said, "That young'un can get into more messes than anyone I've ever seen. Libby never brought home any diseases, she never had scraped knees or climbed trees, or fell down and broke toes, or ran in the fields like an animal. She's a little lady, everybody says so."

First off, she was plump, with blonde, curly hair and eyes as big as saucers, blue too but different blue than mine. I had black hair, with funny blue eyes, so blue they showed every feeling I had. People commented on my eyes, especially those that shook their head and touched me on the head. I figured it was 'cause I had orphan eyes. Besides that I was tall and skinny for my age, with awful freckles on my nose. Grandma rubbed but-

109

termilk all over my face, saying, "That will take them freckles away. It'll bleach them right off." But it didn't.

For some reason, when Grandpa wanted something done, he always called me. "Saire", that's how he pronounced Sara, "stock them can goods on the shelf, or flatten out them boxes, or git a broom and sweep up this here floor." But I didn't mind, 'cause Grandpa let me fill the candy bins and I ate until I didn't want candy for another month or two. I reckon he knew it would make me sick if I ate enough, and I'd stop sneaking pieces. Libby never took candy from the bin. Maybe just orphans did that.

Aunt Ada kept me busy when Grandpa didn't. She said, "Sara, help Libby with her arithmetic. She don't understand it."

"Nothing to understand," I said, "just adding and subtracting, and multiplying."

"Well, maybe the teacher ain't learnin' her."

"Nobody can learn her. She has to learn herself. The teacher just teaches," I said.

"Well, you just go ahead and show her how and don't be so smart-alecky."

"Oh, I'll show her. I wasn't trying to be smart-alecky. I just know the teacher can't learn you."

"Well, you can. I'll give you a nickel every time you learn her something. You can go over to old Erie's drug store and git you one of them ice creams."

"You don't need to do that Aunt Ada. I love helping Libby." And I did. Everyone wanted to help Libby. She was soft and cuddly and sweet.

Anyway, Aunt Ada, who was a real friendly soul sometimes, and Grandpa's daughter-in-law besides, liked to talk to the customers that came in the store. She loved to show off her three kids who were always neat and clean, and never brought home diseases. They stood in a row and she'd say, "This here is Libby, Dolly and Junior," while I leaned on my broom and watched.

One day a real fancy-dressed lady, wearing a big, floppy hat and white gloves, came into the store. She pranced around feeling the tomatoes and inspecting the fruit. We were all there watching, me, as usual, pretty scraped up, and the three other kids all starched and brushed.

I could tell Aunt Ada was dying to be friendly. She lined Libby, Dolly and Junior up and stood behind them, twisting one of Libby's curls. I just stood to the side.

The lady said, "What nice children. Are they yours?" I knew she wasn't speaking of me, so I grinned and watched. Everybody could tell I was an orphan.

Aunt Ada smiled at the lady and answered, "Oh, yes indeedie. I've been wanting to ask a nice lady like you a question."

"What would you like to ask?" the lady inquired, looking puzzled.

"Which of these two girls is the prettiest, the one with the blonde curls or the black-haired one?"

The woman looked at me and then she looked at Libby. "Well," she said, "I don't rightly know, Ma'am, but that tall one with the black hair kinda' looks like you."

Grave Water

Third Place Fiction

The heat had set in early. Already the smell of the river hung in the air like an omen. Trinket knew the river was speaking to her as she and Nikel made their way down River Road. They passed empty fields to the west that would be thick with sugar cane in the winter. On the east side of the road, the river oozed thick and slow, concealed from view by stands of live oak and water oak which grew up to the edge of the levee, rising up behind in a great wave.

It was past nine and the church traffic had already passed this way. They had the road to themselves. They moved like apparitions, in and out of the shadows of the oaks that lined the road. Trinket's long white skirt swept the ground above her bare feet. Her white blouse and head scarf flashed when she emerged from the shadows into the morning light and then back into shadow.

Trinket crossed to the cane field where a stand of wild plum trees huddled, heavy with yellow fruit. Birds had bitten every plum. Hungry flies and gnats swarmed to the bounty. Several long branches hung low, completely shrouded in cocoons. They had been wriggling with caterpillars in July, but now were empty except for the skeletons of branches and leaves. Trinket tore into the thick sides and rolled shreds of cocoon into balls. She dropped them into the pocket of her apron.

She turned, crossed back to the shady side of the road with a sweep of her skirt, and picked up her pace. She scanned the shady distance for some sign of St. John's Cemetery, which had been nestled under the sheltering oaks along the levee as long as anyone alive could remember.

Nikel trailed behind, switching her burden from one hand to the other, finally draping it over her shoulder. She seemed to disappear completely in the shadows in her brown cotton dress, which swayed around her shins. In the light, her face glistened with perspiration. Braids protruded from

her head at every angle and bounced wildly as she stomped along the road
behind her mother. She felt the dampness spreading across her back where
the sack weighed down heavy, and flipped it to her other shoulder, loudly
clinking the bottles and other assorted items inside.

Trinket stopped abruptly, turned and waited for Nikel to catch up.

"Nikel, quit bouncin' that sack, you gone break them bottle!"

"But that ole sack heavy, Momma, and it hot, too," Nikel said, putting
the sack down on the edge of the road and crossing her arms.

Trinket dabbed the perspiration from her forehead with her apron and
stood eyeing Nikel. She adjusted her necklace of assorted keys, beads, but-
tons and magic bags and waited for Nikel to pick up the sack. Finally, Trinket frowned, walked over and retrieved the sack from the ground herself.

"A big twelve years old girl can't carry no little ole sack?" she scolded.

"But it heavy, Momma," Nikel repeated, but more softly now as she
looked at her mother, taking in the angry eye her momma cast on her. She
looked away into the shadows and without looking at her momma said,
"Mr. Rollo say your magic so strong you can make cripple peoples walk.
Why you don't make this ole sack walk? It too heavy to carry."

Tricket turned her around by her shoulder and pointed to a sweeping
oak limb overhead.

"You see that oak switch up there?"

Nikel looked in the general direction and nodded.

"I make that oak switch walk all over you if you back talk me again, girl!
Now we almost to the cemetery, so quit your hollerin' and come on!"

With that, Trinket turned and started down the road again toward the
cemetery. Nikel followed slowly to give her momma's anger a little more
room. She had seen her momma turn cotton mouths and moccasins as stiff
as sticks with just a word. If she told them to get stiff and not bite, that's
what they did. If someone got cut bad and she told them not to bleed, they
didn't. There ain't no good reason, she thought, why she don't make that
ole sack carry itself.

The gravel road into the cemetery was cool in the shade of the oaks that
hovered above the graves in every direction. The graveyard loomed like a
ghost town in the twilight created by the sheltering trees. Graves had been
built above ground for a hundred years due to the unpredictable nature of
the river. Some were as small as Dutch ovens, made of brick and painted
white or silver, with headstones set in at the ends. Others seemed as big as
houses, fashioned from granite or marble, with every manner of decora-
tion and adornment.

Stone flower vases, urns, angels and crosses of every sort appeared here
and there among the graves. The vases and urns were of special interest to

Trinket, as this was her best source of grave water, a critical ingredient for potent magic.

Cicadas dropped their song into every available space until all the trees hummed with them. The song would begin with a burst of energy then wind down until it was almost as quiet as the shade. An occasional bird called. Another would answer, then grow quiet as the cicadas began another vibrating song. Trinket stood motionless, her eyes taking in the canopy of oaks. She listened to the occasional bird chatter as the cicada song came and went. Nikel silently watched her momma survey the scene, knowing that her momma knew what the birds had to say.

Trinket looked to the edges of the cemetery. She followed the line of the wrought iron fence that ran along the road into the shady distance where the oldest graves stood. Then she looked to the levee which rose up behind the cemetery some distance away. She set the sack down on the edge of the gravel path. She opened it carefully and withdrew two blue bottles, put them on the ground, then felt around in the sack until she found the sponges. She handed a bottle and sponge to Nikel, who was familiar with the ritual.

"You go on over to the Judge grave. It got easy water there."

Nikel took the items and walked the short distance to the Judge's grave, which rose up in a grand marble spire. It was flanked on each side by sad angels who, it seemed to Nikel, must be looking round for him. At the front of the monument stood a large marble urn with a wide mouth and curly handles. Nikel raised her dress above her knees and knelt in front of the urn. It contained abundant water. Nikel carefully skimmed the oak leaves from the surface of the water as she had been taught. When the water was clear, she began dipping her sponge into it, careful not to disturb the green fuzz that clung to the inside edge of the urn. As she wrung the contents of the sponge into the mouth of the bottle, grave water ran down her arm and dripped from her elbow on to her brown dress, where it seemed storm cloud patterns began to appear. She gazed at the carvings and intricate swirling letters of the Judge's name carved smoothly into the marble surface. She spoke softly as she repeated the rhythm of dipping and squeezing the sponge.

"I'm taking your water, Judge. Lord know you ain't got no use for it, and they peoples be needin' it, Momma say."

She paused, checked the level of the water in the bottle and resumed her conversation with the Judge.

"Yes sir, this one fine grave your peoples put up for you, uh huh."

She reached up and touched the cool marble, leaving prints in the fine green shadow that clung to the surface of the stone.

Could use some cleaning though, she said, looking at the progress of the lichen and mold that inched across the surface.

"Ain't nobody for that now. Momma say your chirren be over in Baton Rouge and don't come over here no more."

Several sharp blasts from a tug horn broke the cool air, silencing the cicadas and causing Nikel to snatch her hand away from the grave stone. Nikel looked toward the levee, beyond which she imagined the tug, pushing its long flat load along the river's muddy surface. She looked back toward the tall column in the center of the cemetery, where she had left Momma filling her own bottle. There was Trinket with one hand on her hip. Her other arm flailed about as she seemed to shake an angry finger toward a snowy egret that sat inspecting her from the top of the column.

Nikel's bottle was full now. She wiped the sides with her dress, rose and walked toward her mother. As she moved closer, she began to hear her mother's words to the bird.

"Ain't no need to go callin' no names round here, you soul snatcher! They's all asleep except mines and she ain't goin'!"

Nikel froze in her tracks, suddenly sure that the soul snatcher had come for her. She eyed the road in the distance. Maybe she should run, but surely he would catch her if that was his desire. The bird turned its head toward Nikel. She felt its cold eyes on her face, where sweat began to gather, and the bottle of grave water began to shake in her hands.

Trinket followed the bird's stare to Nikel, shaking in the shadows. She slowly backed away from the bird and stood in front of her. One hand reached behind to pull Nikel close while the other clutched the magic bags hanging around her neck and held them up toward the messenger.

"You already done snatch one of mines," Trinket shouted up to the bird. "Ain't no more here for you!" The bird listened, taking it in as far as she could see. It seemed to lose interest. It straightened its feathers with its sharp beak, emitted a series of squawks and clicks, and leaped into the air.

Nikel hollered and clung to her mother, expecting to feel the bird's boney feet latching hold of her hair and carrying her away. But when she opened her eyes, the bird had risen above the oaks, swept over the levee and disappeared. When Nikel found her voice again, she looked into her mother's face, creased by some troubling news. She touched her hand. Trinket looked at her, but was still far away.

"What he say, Momma? That ole soul snatcher come for me?"

Trinket slowly absorbed her question as her thoughts settled back upon her. She spoke softly and touched Nikel's face. " That snatcher ain't studyin' you, child."

Trinket's eyes rolled upward as she lifted her face into the canopy above. Her arms rose straight out like she might fly herself. She began to spin around slowly, speaking in soft secret tones.

"Bird say, his helpers on the way. They be scoopin' eight souls out the river today." She stopped abruptly in mid-spin and looked toward the river. She and Nikel watched silently as eight pelicans glided without a sound, along the levee toward town.

Letting Johnny Go

Third Place Essay

A fulfilling life is one that is full of changes, and therefore, never dull or boring. That sounds so simple and seems so obvious... until we realize that change means letting go of the way things are.

How many times have I heard the nagging reminder, "You're going to have to let go sometime?" My ready reply has always been, "Yes, I know and I will, but it's not going to be easy."

The pain of letting go has been most poignant to me as the mother of my first "boy" child. Every change in his life has required me to step back and let him grow. Sometimes I did so cheerfully and bravely, like when I took him as a three-year old to Kiddie Kollege.

Other times I did it maturely and reassuringly as on his first day of real school. I can still feel the tightness of his squeeze on my hand as we walked toward the smiling nun who was to be his first grade teacher. In those days the teaching sisters wore traditional black and white habits, a sight that was mysterious not only to my son, but also to me. When it was time for him to register at junior high in a new town, it was an off-hand, "You're coming too, aren't you, Mom?" Every fiber of my being responded, "Of course I am!"

Often, letting Johnny go meant that I had to bite my tongue and not protest when his clothes were sloppy or his hair was a mess. I didn't want to interfere with the toughening process, so I just smiled and shrugged when he took risks playing sports or riding his current vehicle and became skillful. I was admirably calm on the outside each time we met in the emergency room, while my motherly instincts were silently screaming, "My baby's hurt! Please, God, protect him a little bit better."

The most difficult times were the transitions. When Johnny turned nine years old, I cried as I realized that half of his years with me were already past. As he packed and prepared to go away to college, I cut and sewed for a solid month to make him a corduroy quilt for his lonely bed. I can still feel the lump in my throat that caused the air to come up in gasps each time he rubbed my sore neck or showed the quilt off to a pal.

No one ever taught me how to let go gracefully, but that's what I'm supposed to be preparing for now. I remember my own mother calling me up after I'd been married for about a month and asking me if I wanted "to come home now" that I'd had a chance to play house for a while.

In four months, my "man" child will be married, and to ensure the success of this union, I must step back and push him forward with pride and glee before the watchful eyes of far too many.

This time it will be different, however, because I've let Johnny go often enough in his life that he is now grown and ready to let me go. For that I am thankful and extremely proud.

Maxwell's Crossing

Honorable Mention Poetry

I remember watching fireflies
dart against the dark in my back yard,
the Milky Way above
loose and unbounded —
a spilling of light

I remember seeing the stars
across the canopied sky at Maxwell's Crossing
you held my hand in your soul
and I knew we'd never be lovers
but always in love with the thought

now lights pollute
the night sky in my back yard
I can see nothing fainter
than the moon itself above the horizon

I remember your breakfast
cooked over a gas flame
it filled my soul as
the sun rose in your kitchen curtains

The Hand of Hattie Flowers

Honorable Mention Fiction

Momma had always gone to Hattie Flowers when it was time for her to labor, because Miss Hattie not only had the gift of birthing, but she also had the gift of listening. My Momma loved babies almost as much as Miss Hattie, and as soon as her last one was walking on its own, Momma was making another trip for another listening.

There are twelve children in my family, including me. We didn't have anything to do with the colored people except for the twenty-four times in the course of Momma's life that she went out to the Flowers' place. That sounds like a lot of visiting with people you don't see that much of, but it takes two visits to bring a baby into this world: one when a woman knows she's with child and she goes for her listening, and a second time when it's time to be delivered. Without exaggeration, Miss Hattie was the best mid-wife in these parts.

Almost without exception, it was expected that every woman would have her day at Miss Hattie's, for the laying on of hands as it was called, and me and my sisters would likewise have our day. I had been married less than a year when my day came. I was going to have a baby. Thank you, Sweet Jesus.

I will admit I was afraid the day I went out there, to the outskirts of town. Oh, I felt safe enough because I knew the way like the back of my hand from all the trips I had made with Momma. Her last reassuring hug didn't calm the flutters that flew around inside me, and I could hardly look her in the eyes. She said, "Don't you hang your head and act all ashamed when you're heading out to Miss Hattie's. You hear me? Every woman in this town has been out there at least once. Don't be afraid, 'cause the Lord's with you." Making an uneasy beeline down Main Street, I waved at every familiar face I knew, and even waved at some I barely recognized, hoping all that waving was showing my confidence, when in reality it was helping me gird my sagging mettle. Even though every wave and every returned smile should have smoothed my way, I was still afraid, afraid because it was my first time, and my Momma wasn't there. I'd take a step, a step, a step, and every ten or so I'd say, "Sweet Jesus, be with me." This would give me the courage to lift my head, smile and then wave at someone, any-one, as my heart pounded against my insides and I made my way through town.

As I stepped off the end of the sidewalk at the edge of town and crossed over the train tracks, my fear vanished. Though I was the only white girl, the only white person around, I was no longer scared. I knew where I was going and everyone knew why I was there. The older women stood smil-ing, understanding the joy of motherhood that swelled inside me, and the girls my age stared in silent wonder, and the little ones ran up beside me saying, "I knows where you're goin'," trailing behind me till their Mommas shooed them away telling them to mind their p's and q's.

I rounded the corner of Miss Hattie's house and knocked on the open side door. The room was dimly filled with honey-colored light. "Come on in, chile." I saw Miss Hattie's thin body walk passed a window. She reached out towards me, and without thinking, I stepped in.

Once inside, inside the birthing room, we sat down, sat down real close. Miss Hattie tucked the hem of her faded dress between her legs, and sitting knee to knee I could feel the softness of its fabric on my own bare calves. She took my hand in hers and laid her other hand on my belly. Her hands were hot. She told me that today was a special day for me and all I had to do was "sit and be with me for a while." As my eyes closed, she pressed her forehead to mine and she began to listen. I don't know if she did this with everyone, 'cause all the women who go to her keep their listenings to themselves. What Miss Hattie does, and what Miss Hattie says, you keep to yourself.

She and I sat silent, so silent for so long. All I could hear was her deep, regular breathing. She sat so long and so still I thought she had gone to sleep, but as soon as that thought had crossed my mind she sat upright, got up from her chair and said, "I's sorry, I didn't hear nothing." My heart fell into my lap. "But don'chu worry, I felt that baby move, everythin's goin' to be alright. Sometimes they's voice is so small, even I has a hard time hearin' them." I sat there not knowing what to do. And then, "I'll see you again when your time's come." And Hattie Flowers disappeared into the shad-ows.

Well, she had been right. My time went fine. My baby grew and moved and kicked inside me, and I had my first healthy baby girl thanks to Miss

Hattie. Any fears of that silent voice passed and my family rejoiced at her birth.

***

Momma always told us kids that she had had twelve children because there had been twelve apostles. Not that we were named after them, and not that they were our patron saints or anything like that, but she told us that if it was good enough for our Lord to have twelve companions, then it was good enough for her and Daddy. So when Momma brought each of us home, or so the story goes, and she'd lay us down to sleep for the first time in our new home, she'd say a thank you prayer and end it with something like, "Well, Lord, that's number so and so, and x-number more to go" (as if the Lord didn't already know how many He had sent their way). Then she'd whisper in our ear the name of our apostle and that would send us into the most heavenly sleep, or so she said.

As we got older and learned our Bible lessons, we learned about the Lord's twelve, learned their names, and learned what kind of men they were. And just like clockwork, a certain Sunday would roll around and Momma always knew who had learned about Judas in Sunday School that day, and learned about the betrayal of our Lord and Savior. That someone would sit silently at the supper table and worry, worrying that they had been given the name of the betrayer Judas Iscariot, worrying themselves sick until they asked, "Is it me, Momma? Am I Judas 'Scariot?" Being children, we were afraid that that name would bring upon us some kind of bad luck; but neither Momma nor Daddy ever fessed up to the order of the apostles in relation to the order of our births. Besides, "Jesus loved Judas just as much as He loved any of the others," just as she and Daddy loved each of us, equal and the same. Knowing Momma as I did, I figured she would leave Judas until the last. Since I was born luckily somewhere toward the front end of us twelve, I knew I was safe, but then you never know; and it was this "you never know" that has always made me wonder and worry just a little bit.

I wasn't about to have twelve children, so as new parents we decided three was a good Godly number. I think it's said large families beget small families, and since we didn't plan to carry on Momma and Daddy's apostle tradition, I decided instead to count the days, count off the apostles for the first twelve days of each of my babies' lives, and then to make extra good on it, the first twelve years of their lives as well, as they grew older; then maybe 1 of my three would dare do as Momma and Daddy had done and have their own twelve children, Lord have mercy if they dared.

And so I began my own apostle tradition. On the first day as a sliver of sunlight cut between the curtains, I stood beside the crib, and barely mov-

122

ing my lips so as not to waken her, I started, "Andrew, for he is said to be the first, the first called to be beside Jesus." And on the second day, "Simon Peter, who was Andrew's brother, who was the second," and right on down the line, each morning a new apostle stood guard around her crib. On day twelve, as I walked to the crib, my baby moved, then fussed a bit and then broke into a wailing cry. As I tried to comfort her, I whispered, "I have another apostle for you, but fear not, for Jesus loved him too, for he had been likewise chosen." She calmed in my arms. "Happy 12th day on earth, today is called Judas, and he too is loved; and there will be many, many more wonderful days, thanks to God and Miss Hattie."

But as the months passed, she began having earaches, having them more often than not. They were earaches that left her red-faced and crying and burning with fever. The doctor's drops and creams and compresses brought her no comfort, no cures. We passed a year full of office visits, medicines and infections, until a doctor from the next town suggested surgery. He wanted to put a tube into each eardrum to let them heal from the inside out. With time the tubes would fall out by themselves and she'd be past the age of earaches.

That's what they did. They operated on those tiny eardrums, on my baby's tiny eardrums; and within days she was smiling again and sleeping through till morning. The neighbors would stop at our porch each evening and we'd share in the night's newfound quietness.

It was during that spring, a spring of cooing days and gentle nights, when the time for my third visit to Miss Hattie came upon me. This listening let me bring my youngest sister along so she could hold the baby while Miss Hattie and I sat knee to knee; so she could lay her hand on me and listen; so we could sit with our foreheads pressed together. As I spent my time with her, I listened, too. I listened so hard. I listened but I couldn't even hear Miss Hattie's breathing this time.

We were so still, me waiting, her listening; then I felt something drop upon my hand. Was it a drop of sweat? The room had become so very still and so very hot. And then another, and then out of the room's silence, the smallest sob slipped from Hattie's lips. She sat back and wiped tears from the wells beneath her eyes. "Don't worry, chile, I'm cryin' with joy. I heard it this time. I heard a child cryin', a newborn baby cryin'. The voice — it's so beautiful, it's like an angel callin'."

Now that's exactly what I wanted to hear — a crying, happy baby. Thank you, Sweet Jesus, there was no silence this time in the birthing room as I stepped outside into the summer sun, smiling at the two who sat patient, waiting for me on the steps of Miss Hattie's home.

The four of us — me, my sister, and my two babies, the one in my arms and the perfect one inside me — the four of us rushed home to tell Momma that everything was going to be better than ever. Hardly a block towards home, and giddy with news and filled with hope, I was suddenly stopped — no, taken by a bright light. The air around me became white, as white as a whitewashed wall. Then a wind rushed down upon me and forced me to look up and stare into the sun. Almost as quickly something covered my burning eyes, a hand, a wing, a veil passed overhead making the sun fly through it like light through the spokes of a wagon wheel. A golden chariot wheel high up in the sky. And there in the heart of that heavenly wheel I saw my little girl's face, and then water — no, more like rain, rain began flowing from her ears, and the rain streamed down and shone in the sunlight, flowing down like tears, tears running down her cheeks, water weeping forth from her tiny ears. Then I heard someone crying, the angels crying, calling and quickening me to convince the doctors to take those things out of my baby's ears. And in a blink my sister, my babies and I broke into a run as the tears fell down, fell down around us forming large wet circles on the pavement beneath our feet, huge dark teardrops falling around us as we crossed onto our own side of the tracks.

When I told the doctors that it was time for them to unstop her ears, they said it was too soon and the period of danger hadn't passed. I insisted I was right. I told them over and over until I could no longer remember what I had said, but all the while I talked all I could see was my baby's face up there in the clouds and her tears of joy flowing down upon the earth. Then in a moment of silence, they listened; and I was right. Her ears healed up as quick as lightning. Sweet Jesus, you have made my child whole again and we all shall sleep soundly, safely encircled in Thy arms. From that night on I'd hold my little one to me, her ear upon my belly, listening to her new baby sister quickening inside me. How I longed to see Miss Hattie once again.

In the last week of December, Miss Hattie birthed my second child, another girl who came into this world crying — but crying this time like she had said, like an angel, and so we named her Angelique. Miss Hattie's girl who helped in the birthing room said the name reminded her of a princess or a Hollywood movie star.

"Donchu go bein' disrespectful to God. We're here doin' His work, not talkin' about some picture show. Now, go on, an' gather up our new mama's things."

"Miss Hattie, thank you, and may God continue to bless the house of Flowers."

"The house of Flowers," she repeated, rolling the sweetness of those words around in her mouth, and softly sighed, "I likes that." Then she ran her dark thumb over the rosy brow of her most recent birth, then once again, making the sign of the cross.

"My little Angelique. You've picked a glorious name, an' between you an' me, I must say, it's a glamorous name, too." And with that, Momma helped me on home.

***

Angelique. Disrespectful or not, she certainly was the star in our household.

"That's two down and ten to go, you'd best catch up." Momma was sure I was working on my own set of twelve since the first two came so quick, but I never had the nerve to tell her I didn't want that many children, three young'uns was the limit. The limit. The limit. Next time around we wanted a boy, but that wasn't planned to happen for quite a while. Besides I had my apostle tradition in place and didn't need no troop of twelve crowding my dinner table.

I slipped into the babies' room. All I could hear was the soft suck of their breaths as they slept. The simplest sleep; a sister long waited for; now so close by. Over the two cribs hung pictures, identical pictures framed in gold, frames as gold as the streets of heaven, pictures of our Lord's last supper; Him surrounded by His friends, His apostles. Leaning over Angelique's crib, I pointed to Andrew and whispered, "That's Andrew. He's for your first morning. Andrew, the first to be beside Jesus."

And every morning thereafter I'd go in to see Angelique and tell her the apostle of the day. Not that she or her sister knew what I was saying, or even who these fellows were, but I knew my little ones were being watched over just the same by the mention of our Savior's chosen men.

I don't want to say for obvious reasons, but I had left Judas, like before, till the end. I am my mother's daughter, and we're much too much alike.

"Momma? I've been thinking about this apostle thing. Did any of us kids, you know, the one of us who was... who was "given" to Judas... did they ever have any problems afterwards? I mean like poor health, or trouble sleeping, or grinding their teeth? I mean —"

"Don't be silly. That would be more a superstition than trusting in the good Lord. Right?"

"Well, I've also asked the preacher, and he says God wouldn't send suffering down on a child just because someone had mentioned Judas' name in their presence. But doesn't it seem, you know, a coincidence?"

"Now listen to me. Your Daddy and I never would have done something that would have brought harm to any of you kids. And you aren't either. The preacher knows what he's talking about, so leave it at that."

And so I did. It was a new year, a new baby, and a renewed faith. A late rising winter sun crept over the horizon as I crept into my daughters' room.

It was day twelve, and freed of that silly superstition, I singled out Judas sitting at the right hand of Jesus; his flaming red hair; his steadfast stare; staring, questioning, wondering if he was Christ's betrayer. My fingertip touched the chest of Judas.

"That's Judas Iscariot, he too was loved by Jesus."

As I leaned down to kiss my angel, her cheek was cold, as cold as the glass in the golden frame, as cold as the spot where I had touched his face. Judas Iscariot's face. He who sits unmoving. He who sits stock-still, asking, wanting, needing to know, "Is it me, Lord?" Then a blade of sunlight cut between the curtains and plunged into my heart.

***

A tiny white casket with white embossed roses. A closed coffin. From sleep into eternal sleep. Two parents devastated. A little sister barely understanding why she wasn't going to have the sister she had been promised. And all those people. Strangers. Strangers to a child not even twelve days old. So many grown-ups all dressed in black, all dressed in black keeping vigil over a tiny white casket covered with white embossed roses.

***

It's been a year since the angels cried for Angelique. Miss Hattie had been wrong. Two listenings gone wrong and I wasn't ever going back to see that woman again. All she's doing is some kind of magic, and her doctoring is all wrong, too. She had done something to my baby. She had put a mark upon her head. I was not going back, ever, to see that woman.

Hardhearted and angry, feeling the strength of my adulthood, I blasphemed that woman and all she had done to me. But Momma said I had to make that trip again.

"You have to go back," she said, "and apologize for all you've been saying behind Miss Hattie's back. She's meant no harm to you or your babies. She's the best midwife around here. She's got the gift. The touch. The problem is you didn't listen to her, not the other way around. You must go see her again. For if you don't, it's not only Angelique, but it's you, too, who is dead."

Momma walked me to the place where the sidewalk ends. I stepped off the pavement at the edge of town and walked across the train tracks. I was going back, but against my will. Sure, I was going back, but I was angry and was going to tell her if she knew so much why didn't she tell me something else, why wasn't she honest, why didn't she warn me, tell me, tell me anything but what she did. Tell me the truth and my baby wouldn't be dead!

As I walked through that section of town, that section of town on the other side of the tracks, that section of town where they have no sidewalks, past all those colored girls, the ones who stared at me with their blackened silence; they who knew I was the one whose baby had died; them. I walked as quickly as my angry feet could carry me to that Flowers woman's house, telling her and telling her again exactly how I felt and that I never, ever, wanted her to lay her hands on me again. And not only was I angry at her, I was angry at every one of those coloreds out there who stood staring. I could see all of them out of the corner of my eye, staring at me as I stared at their dusty, weed-covered street.

As I rounded the corner of the house, digging in my heels, grinding hard the soles of my shoes, making for the steps that lead into her birthing room, there in the doorway stood Miss Hattie Flowers, that small, weak, colored woman. My jaw clenched tight. I wanted to accuse her of such ungodly, unpure things. And I stood there. Clenched tight. Clenched so tight tears welled up in my eyes. Then she stepped towards me. How dare she. She took my hand in hers, pressed her forehead to mine, laid her hot hand upon my belly, and I listened.

Memories

Honorable Mention Non-fiction

The year was 1961. I was on my way to college. I had my choice of going to an all girl's school in Georgia or going to Florida State University in Tallahassee. I chose FSU. It was agreed that I could go to FSU if I could pay the out-of-state tuition myself. Since I had worked my last three years of high school, I could afford to do this. I had one brother going to University of Florida and another brother going to the University of Georgia. I had no idea at the time how much of a sacrifice my parents were making by having three children in college at the same time.

So, there I was away from home for the first time. Of course I had to go to the sorority rush parties and to every fraternity party that I could. I was sure that my parents would want me to broaden my horizons. I got pledged to a terrific sorority — Phi Mu. I was certain my parents would not be-grudge me the opportunity to enjoy my new sisterhood. I wrote my first letter home:

Dear Mom and Dad,

I know you will be thrilled to hear that I have pledged Phi Mu Sorority. It won't cost that much more per month since I can eat at the sorority house and I now have a job grading test papers for one of my professors. I also want you to know that I have started smoking. I know I shouldn't! I know it's not good for me, but everyone in my dorm smokes and the only way I can stay in my room is to smoke. It's in self-defense!! I just didn't want to feel like I was doing something behind your back.

Love,
Your Phi Mu daughter,
Carol

P.S. I have met the most wonderful guy. His name is Joe. I'm sure you will just love him. I have a ride home this weekend. See you late Fri. night.

Within a week of my first visit home I received my first letter from my father:

November 12, 1961

Dear Sorority Girl:

This is my first chance to write to you since your brief visit with us. I want to tell you how wonderful it was to have a sorority girl in the house, particularly a Phi Mu. This is something that every parent should experience during the course of their normally dreary and uneventful lives. I can assure you that your sorority affiliation has made many changes in our way of living. Three people stopped me on the street yesterday and asked me if I wasn't a sorority girl's father — one of them even guessed that I was a Phi Mu's father. Many more cast admiring glances in my direction. I have been practicing walking around with my head high in the air as you told me to. I am going to have to give this up for a little while though until my leg heals. I am afraid I overdid it and ran into a chair. However, this is only a temporary setback and I expect to resume practice within the next week or so.

Mother is dieting again as she was able to achieve only 80% effectiveness in her efforts to assume a proud bearing. We are all agreed that the unresponsive 20% simply has to go.

Your little brother's teacher informs us that he has "great potential" — for what, we are not sure. Actually, I think she is a little puzzled by his performance, particularly since she knows he is a Phi Mu's brother and has been expecting wonderful things from him. As yet we haven't had the heart to tell her of his Sig Ep connections since we thought David could overcome this handicap without the teacher becoming aware of it.

Tiger, our feline member of the family, hardly even speaks to the other cats in the neighborhood anymore, with the exception of one or two that come from sorority families. Some people seem to think that his interest lies in the fact that these particular cats are females. I am personally inclined to discount this theory. Tiger, being a cat of the world and wise beyond his years, is undoubtedly aware of the fine distinction between Greek and independent, and I am sure that his association is based upon these less earthy considerations.

The people at the bank are about the only ones who are not impressed with our Phi Mu status. They continue to be nasty and unreasonable every time mother overdraws her account. However, in view of the many other benefits of being a sorority family we consider this only a minor irritation.

> *Love,*
> *Your "POOR" but proud father*

P.S. There is a message in this letter.

Our letters crossed in the mail. As I read my father's letter, I assumed that he was reading mine. I might have waited to send my letter if I had thought he might not appreciate more unpleasantness until he recuperated from my last letter. I wasn't totally thoughtless!

Dear Mom and Dad,

Just thought I should let you know that I got two "pink slips" this semester. I can't imagine why, since about all I do is go to work and study. I promise I will cut down on my dating to once a week and only party on the weekends. I will bring up my grades!

Love from your extremely, hard-working, one and only daughter,

Carol

I went into greater detail but that was the gist of my letter. Within a few days I received my second letter from my Dad, which again showed his great sense of humor (with a touch of sarcasm thrown in).

November 16, 1961
Dear "Student":

The word "student" above is used in the loosest possible sense of the word. I have just finished reading your recent letter about "pink slips" in which you devote pages to explaining how hard you are studying, how you can't understand what is happening, and that you would probably crack up at any moment from overwork. I couldn't sleep all night just worrying about you. I am glad to hear that you are blaming yourself instead of the teachers for a change, and your assurances to do better are noted with gratification.

All of this has an old familiar ring, and I seem to have heard this recording before. As a matter of fact, it's been played so many times it's getting scratchy. Maybe we should turn it over and see what's on the flip side. I have been curious about this for some time.

You mention that you have cut down to one date a week. Just how many were you having before this????? In other words, just how much of a sacrifice are you making????? We have had a little discussion and several solutions have been offered. One of these is to get you married off and quit worrying about you (older brother No.1). Another is that I should take my name off your birth certificate (nameless friend). Another is an all girl's school (guess who?). Another one, which I think is rather drastic, is that you settle down and tend to business. Actually, I can't see how a girl like you, with a brilliant father, a hardworking mother, and three stupid brothers, can make such a mess of things.

Seriously though, we have faith in you, and being somewhat gullible, we are inclined to believe you when you say things will be different. The only thing I want to know is whether they are going to get better or worse. We love our little daughter (one and only) and want her to finish college even if it does take ten years.

Love,
from your gullible ex-father

Meanwhile, I was sure that I was totally in love with Joe. I knew that I wanted to marry him and spend the rest of my life with him. I went home with him for a couple of days during the Christmas holidays and met his family, then we went up to Georgia for him to meet my family. We decided to elope at the end of January and not tell our parents until the summer break when they would have adjusted to the fact that we were a serious item. Well, this scheme did not work. Soon after we were married, I discovered that I was pregnant. This naturally scared me to death since now I would have to face my parents not only with the fact of my marriage, but also with their impending grandparent status.

We went to my home during Spring Break and broke the news to my family. They were both crushed, since I was their only daughter and they had always wanted me to have a traditional wedding with my father walking me down the aisle. My mother was wonderful and a real trooper. She hugged me and welcomed Joe to the family. She and I both cried our eyes out, and she then said to please try not to get pregnant until I finished school. I started to bawl all over again when I told her that her advice was a little late. My father was so hurt that he went to his room and did not speak to me during the rest of our visit. My mother said to give him time to adjust to the situation, so I went back to school with a heavy heart and waited to hear from my Dad. Finally, one long month later, with no other communication from my father since my fateful visit home, this letter arrived:

May 29, 1962
Dear Carol,

I have just finished figuring up the amount of money we are going to save, and you and Joe now have our blessings and sympathy on your marriage. Joe also has our best wishes for luck and prosperity, both of which he will need.

I gave Mother your message about the November 5th schedule and the kicking which was to start in two weeks. I hope that He, She, or It as the case may be, kicks the daylights out of you.

Mother came home from the hospital Sunday and is doing fine. At the moment she is a little peeved with the doctor and me. He came in after the operation and apologized to me for taking so long, and made some remark about her being a little stout. I was indiscreet enough to repeat this conversation to your mother. I think some good may come of it, though, since she is finally determined to do something about her weight. In fact, mother is planning on going to a reducing salon, and buying some new clothes (which we can now afford). There is also some talk about a new car and going to college this fall. I am not sure that I am up to all this, but I intend to keep a close watch on her, particularly if she starts college. I think Mother has some inherent playgirl tendencies which are about to come out. One playgirl steps out of the ranks, and another steps right in to take her place (I assume you know that your playing days are over and that you are about to have a serious look at life).

With regard to the cooking lessons, I think it would be best for you to practice on Joe. He is young, strong, and deserving. If you feel that you love Joe too much and want to practice at home, we can let you use your two older brothers and the cat as guinea pigs. There are also a couple of dogs around here that we consider to be nuisances. If all this is successful, we can probably spread the operation into other neighborhoods.

I have dyed my hair gray, pinched wrinkles in my face, slowed down to half pace, and walk all stooped over. In spite of this, I still don't feel like a prospective grandfather. I think we had better face up to it — I am not ready! In view of this it would be best to call the whole thing off.

Mother is having a lovely time telling all of her friends and neighbors about her wayward daughter. It is quite interesting watching them perk up and start counting on their fingers when the baby part is mentioned. There is nothing like an unorthodox marriage and an early pregnancy to arouse speculation. Up until now, everybody thought we were pretty dull people. We showed them!!

We have been trying to get both of your older brothers married off, but it is quite difficult to find anyone willing to support them. Oh well, I suppose they will end up graduating before they find a mate.

Why don't you encourage your friends Judy and Patricia to run off and get married so their parents can have some excitement too? I imagine things must be pretty dull for them.

In spite of everything, we still love you. I am enclosing a small check, which should be enough to get you home for a visit. After a week or so of your cooking we shouldn't have any trouble taking up a collection for sending you back to Joe.

Love from your
Father

P.S.(added serious note): You and Joe have our blessings and best wishes. Hope everything works out fine for you.

I have tried to raise my children using humor as my father did

132

with me. This article is dedicated to my mother and my father because I love them very much, and everything that I am today I owe to them. I want them to know that the lessons finally took! All I had to do was have children of my own, and suddenly my parents became the wisest people I ever knew.

Isn't that amazing?

Treasures

Honorable Mention Children's Fiction

Everyone has treasures. I didn't know that for a long time, maybe because I didn't know what a treasure was. I never figured a dried up rose or a yellow butterfly with its wings pinned down to be a treasure like some people. I thought a rose was beautiful while it lived, but then it dried up and withered away. A butterfly would light on a flower for a second, then fly away if it wasn't caught in a net, then it's gone like the rose.

But some people keep dried roses. Grandma does, and you know where? In the Bible. There were two of them, all flattened out, their delicate petals beginning to crumble. I was afraid to touch them. Grandma told me they were treasures to her, but not the same kind of treasure as the mahogany table that was in the parlor with the crystal bowl on the top. Then again, Grandma said everything in the china cabinet was a treasure with all those cut glass bowls and pale, thin china plates and cups and saucers. They would sparkle when the light shone on them, but I was never allowed to touch them. I never went near that china cabinet so I never gave a thought to treasures.

Besides, treasures are not the same with everybody, especially when it comes to boys and girls. Now take my cousin Junior.

One weekend, I was visiting at the farm and Aunt Ada decided we were going to get rid of all the things that had accumulated over a couple of years. Accumulated means stuff you have and never use; stuff that just piles up and is in the way. Well, we started in Junior's room, in the closet. Aunt Ada pulled a shoe box off the shelf and all the stuff fell out. There was a steely; a steely is round like a marble and silver in color. Boys like them because when you play marbles, a steely hits hard because it is like steel and spreads those glass marbles all over the place. Like I said, there was a steely, a dried snake skin, where that came from I'll never know, a baseball with a lot of names written on it, a tie clasp that looked like gold, but who knows, well there were lots of little things that scattered all over the floor.

Aunt Ada said, "Sara, get the broom and sweep up all that junk and dump it in that bag over yonder, then put it in the trash can."

I got the broom and swept it up but I put the stuff back in the shoebox, then I put the shoebox in the bag. I really wanted to look at Junior's special stuff, so I put the bag behind the grape arbor. Then again, I would feel bad if someone threw some of my books out. Maybe Junior loved all those things. I just prayed that Aunt Ada wouldn't ask me if I threw the bag out. What could I say?

Anyway, she was too busy sorting out clothes that Libby and Junior had outgrown. Dolly got Libby's old stuff, and she hated to get hand-me-downs as she called it. Thank goodness I was too tall for Libby's little, rick-rackey dresses. They wouldn't do for me. They were what Grandma would call prissy.

Well, while we were busy carrying and stacking things in piles that were to go to the church or the Salvation Army, Junior came to his room and discovered his things were gone. He yelled, "Mom, where's my shoe box?"

"It's gone. I'm getting rid of junk in this house."

"No, no Mom, those were my treasures," he cried as he ran from the room. Tears clouded his eyes while he struggled to hold them back.

I called to him, "Junior it's all right." That was all I could say. He just yelled back, "Go away Sara."

I wanted to do something but I knew I couldn't, not then anyway, but before I went back to Grandma's house I would put Junior's shoe box back in his room.

Libby and Dolly had some treasures too, but they promised to clean out their dresser drawers on their own. Guess Aunt Ada was tired by the time we got to their room.

Libby had a fur muff and hat that she kept in a secret place in the bottom of the closet. There was a lace handkerchief, an earring and a gold bracelet, even a small, porcelain doll. She let me peek into the box and I was honored that she let me see, but I had to promise never to tell, not even Dolly.

I kinda wished after that that I had some treasures, but then I'd never held dear the things that others thought were treasures. Wish I'd paid more attention instead of always dreaming of being someone beside Sarie as Grandpa called me. I wanted to have a fancy name like Crystal or Sylvia, but when I thought about it, a glittery name wouldn't do for me. I needed a dignified name, maybe Katherine. Not that I ever acted the least bit like a lady, but I could be some day if I worked on it.

There I go again, just dreaming, but I wonder what Grandpa would call a treasure. Next time I had a chance to talk to him, I'd ask him. Before I got around to our talk, I discovered something that was important enough to be a treasure.

I told Grandma about the cleaning spree Aunt Ada had at the farm, and I confessed to her what I'd done about Junior's treasures. Even said out loud that maybe it would be nice to have a treasure.

Grandma didn't say it was right or wrong what I did. She just said no one had a right to throw anothers' things out without permission.

That made me feel better about disobeying Aunt Ada, but then, what do you know? Grandma decided to clean out her dresser drawers.

In a way, it was going to be fun because I'd never been in Grandma's dresser drawers and had no idea what they held. So I sat on the floor by Grandma as she went through one drawer and then the other. She would put things to the side that she intended to get rid of. There was a corset with stays and laces. In case you don't know what a corset is, I'll have to explain. I even had to ask Grandma.

What she told me, made me silly, laughing. Women wore corsets under their dresses to make them look thinner. You wrapped the corset around your belly and laced yourself up, kinda like a shoestring. The tighter you laced, the thinner you looked.

Well, that was one thing in the drawer. Learned something that I'd never read in a book. If you stick around Grandma long enough you'll learn a lot, cause she knows about stuff you'd never dream of.

After Grandma explained about the corset, she took some baby booties out, but they were not to be given away. She held up a black lace shawl that had been wrapped in tissue paper. I could smell a flowery odor, kind of old, and it made me dreamy and silent. I wanted to ask Grandma if that shawl was a special treasure, but I couldn't. Somehow there was a strange expectancy in the room. I almost held my breath as she drew from the bottom drawer a yellow organdy and lace dress. I held my breath and drew near, so delicate, smelling of dead roses. Grandma's face was soft, her eyes teary as she held the dress out to me. She said softly, "This was your mother's. You may keep it now."

It was then that I knew what it meant to have a treasure, and I also understood why Grandma decided to clean out her dresser drawers.

POBox 6502, Destin, Florida 32550
www.emeraldcoastwriters.org

Members of Emerald Coast Writers, Inc.

Board of Directors

Founder & President:	Julia Schuster
Vice President:	Dale Willett
Secretary:	Diane Harris
Treasurer:	Ellen Martin

Committee Chairs

Web Site Liaison:	Darlene Dean
Historian:	Carol Anderson
Writers' Conference Chair:	Philip Turner
Newsletter Editor:	Marguerite Hartt
Young Writers Contest Chair:	Janet Manchon
Press Release Chair:	Judy Winn

Members of Emerald Coast Writers, Inc.

Charter Members

Carol Anderson
Lynn Carol Bowling
Mary Brown
Mahala Church
Wilma Fredrick
Diane Harris
Susan Farish Horn
Arlene Karian

Valerie Lofton
Sue Lutz
Dawn Lyons
Ellen Martin
Delores Merrill
Joan Mucci
Beverly Sassano
Julia Schuster
Gail Shorter

Members

Ronnie Angleus
Kinga Barrarecchia
Xellaine Beith
Lee Betts
Bill Bonner
Cynthia Burton
Tom Corcoran
Armand Coutu
Jerry Cox
Gary Crowther
Darlene Dean
Jennifer DeGregorio
Jack Downing
Audrey Edwards
Anne Fraser
Noel Foster
Melita Gardner
Mary Heinz Garzoni
Rusty Gasparian
Melanie Gibson
Deborah Ganzalez
John Gossage

Frank Guiliano
Felda Marie Harrison
Marguerite Hartt
Anne Hinze
Vicki Hinze
Edward Hogeboom
Joyce Holland
Ellen Holt
Jean Hontz
Collier D. Houston
Neil Howard
Bob Hunt
Alicia Larkin
Janet Manchon
Jane Mayes
Katina Meacham
Kenneth Michel
Robert Newkirk
Alice Paprocki
Millie Pusch
Tonya Rasor
Amy Riddell

Amy Jo Rosarti
Karen Saunders
Ellen Saunders
Kay Schoeppner
Charles Schuster
Dorothy Schweitzer
Carol Miller Scoggins
Pamela Shirkey
Gail Shorter
Walker Sloan
Gilbert R. Stiff, Jr.
Troy Taylor
Lorna Tedder
Philip Turner
Karen VanSleen
David Ward
Jan Whitford
Ray Willcox
Dale Willett
Judy Winn
Bill Winston
Amos Young

Published Authors of Emerald Coast Writers, Inc.

When our organization was first formed, we had no idea of the number of talented, professional writers that were looking for a "home." They are accomplished writers in their own right and are published across numerous genres, including fiction, non-fiction and poetry. Several contribute regularly to newspapers and magazines; some write for e-zines and support sites for writers. It is with great pride we showcase here those members who are published in book-length products.

Co-authors: Bill Bonner and Terri DuLong
Title: *IMMORAL SYMPHONY*
Author Pen Names: Bonner Dulong
Publisher: Gardenia Press
Publication Date: August 2003
A successful surgeon and a senator's assistant find themselves among the homeless in Washington, D.C. Together, they encounter Project 1947 whose goal is deadly control.

Author: Lynn Carol Bowling
Title: *GO YE INTO AFRICA*
Publisher: Prescott Press
ISBN#: 0-933451-12-1
Price: $10.00 Softcover Nonfiction
Recounts the author's missionary experience in Kenya, from everyday dangers of African wildlife to threats of harm from some unhappy natives.
&
Title: *HONOR THY FATHER & MOTHER*
Publisher: Fairway Press
ISBN#: 0-7880-0995-8
Price: $12.00 Softcover Nonfiction
A true-life account of how the author's family dealt with the decisions and devastations of caring for elderly parents.

Author: Audrey Edwards
Title: *EMIL HOLZHAUSER: THE PORTRAIT OF AN ARTIST*
Publihser: CeShore
ISBN#: 1 -58501 - 027-8
Price: $12.95, non-fiction
This biography records the prejudice and hatred directed at Holzhauer, a German/American artist whose paintings now hang in prestigious museums across the USA.

Author: Marie Harrison

Title: *GARDENING IN THE COASTAL SOUTH*
Publisher: Pineapple Press
ISBN#: 1-56164-274-6
Price: $14.95 Softcover Non-fiction
This book is a valuable reference for anyone wishing to learn more about gardening in the Coastal South (USDA Zones 8 and 9).

Author: Marguerite Hartt

Title: *THRIFTING INTO A DEBT-FREE, CAREFREE LIFESTYLE*
Publisher: Universal Publishers
ISBN#: 1-58112-602-6
Price: $14.95 Soft cover Non-fiction - Personal finance
Provides tips for savings on every good and service, including personal stories and examples of avoiding hidden expenditures and achieving a debt-free, rewarding life.

Author: Vicki Hinze

Title: *LADY LIBERTY*
Publisher: Bantam Dell Publishing Group
ISBN# 05-535-83-522
Price: $6.50, Mass Market Paperback
Political Romantic Suspense Thriller. The first female Vice-President has 72 hours to prevent World War III and stop a nuclear distaster.
&
Title: *S.A.S.S.: IN PLAIN SIGHT*
Publisher: Silhouette
ISBN# To be assigned in July, 2003
Price: Not yet established, paperback
Military Romantic Suspense Thriller. A Secret Assignment Security Specialist must discover how the top Intelligence Broker in the world is infiltrating U.S. classified sources, jeopardizing operatives and missions worldwide. www.vickihinze.com

Author: Joyce Holland

Title: *BOAT DOLLIES*
Deadly Alibi Press
ISBN #1-886199-05-1
Sally Malone sails into harbor and partially witnesses the murder of a boat dollie named Rita. Rita's diary reveals that she knew enough to make more than one person on the island a suspect in her macabre death.
&

Title: ***BEYOND GULF BREEZE***
Deadly Alibi Press
ISBN # 1-886199-08-6
Someone is killing the women of Gulf Breeze and wants it to look as though they were abducted by aliens. Sally Malone investigates, encounters evidence of alien visitation, and the dark side of mankind.
&
Title: ***MY, MY, MYRA***
Sex, Lies, Money and Murder on Florida's Emerald Coast
1st Books Library
ISBN # 1-4107-2675-4
A true crime.
Myra Vaivada regularly cruised the island in a limo to pick up men or women to feed her insatiable sexual appetite. Her husband Robert didn't mind, so what made her place a gun to his head and blow his brains out?

Author: Daniel Collier Houston

Title: *Suck A Rock*
Traffore Publishing
ISBN# 1-55369-375-2
$15.95, softcover, Memior
Houston, a.k.a. "Alabama", born in Alabama in 1923, left home in 1939, age 16, hitchhiked to Canada and enlisted in the Canadian Army. Part Cherokee, his grandmother told him that Indians can run 100 miles without food or water by sucking on a rock. This story outlines the 5+ years he fought in WWII.

Author: Neil Howard

Title: ***STUDENT BODY***
Publisher: Lighthouse Press, Inc.
ISBN: 0-97148227-2-1
Price & Type: $13.95, Trade Paperback, Mystery
Tyler Richmond has no intention of making waves as a new faculty member at Stonewater College. His plans are disrupted after the disappearance and death of a beautiful co-ed. If he chooses to pursue the murderer, he could lose his job...or his life!
&
Title: ***HUNTER'S PREY***

Publisher: Lighthouse Press, Inc.
ISBN: 0-932211-01-2
Price & Type: $13.95, Trade Paperback, Mystery/Suspense
Plot: There is a cold-blooded killer hiding in the Virginia forest. Deputy Diane Richmond is determined to catch the elusive marksman. During the hunt, she encounters unspeakable terror. The heart-pounding tension builds as she confronts the greatest challenge of her career.
www.myswriter.com

Author: Dawn Lyons

Title: *THE DRY WELL*
Publisher: Accolade Books
ISBN# 0-972555-80-3
Trade paperback, Literary fiction, see www.dawnlyons.com
An emotionally charged story of a single mother changed forever by a tragic event.

Author: Jane Mayes

Title: *SCENE TO UNSEEN*
Jane Mayes, P.O. Box 292, Port Austin, MI 48467
2001, illus. by author, 59 pp., $8.00.
A collection of 53 poems that lead the reader from the wonders of the world to the realm of the spirit.

Author: Lorna Tedder

Title: *ACCESS*
Publisher: Spilled Candy Publications
ISBN#: 189271812X
Price: $19.95
An End-Times thriller set on the Emerald Coaast and featuring time travel, biological warfare, and reincarnation.
&
Title: *FLYING BY NIGHT*
Publisher: Spilled Candy Publications.
ISBN#: 1892718448.
Price: $16.95
"The last time I saw my two husbands alive, they were standing naked before the Altar of the Goddess....

Author: Audrey K. Wendland

Title: *FLORENCE — the true story of a country schoolteacher in Minnesota and North Dakota*
Publisher: self-published
ISBN #: 0-9728506-0-0
Price: $15.00 plus S&H ($4.50) — can be ordered from my website: www.awendland.com.
Nostalgic tale of the adventures of my mother in the pre-World War I era; the farm families she lived with and the children she taught.

SandScript 2003 - Winning Entries - by Author

Congratulations
Winners!

Blessings,

Vicki

Vicki Hinze

> The next book in Vicki's "Lady" series
> is *Lady Justice*.
> Due out, Summer 2004.
> Bantam Dell Publishing Group.

> The first book in Vicki's new "S.A.S.S."
> series is *In Plain Sight*.
> Due out, Summer 2004.
> Silhouette Publishing Group.

> S.A.S.S.
>
> In
> Plain
> Sight

Vicki Hinze is the award-winning, best-selling author of fourteen novels, with another four currently under contract, a nonfiction book, and over a thousand articles. Her novels have been published in over a dozen countries and foreign languages. She acts as a mentor for over a thousand writers but still considers herself a student of the writing craft.
www.vickihinze.com

149

Printed in the United States
1273900006BA/79-402